BEING A CHRISTIAN WITHOUT BEING AN IDIOT!
11 ASSUMED TRUTHS THAT MAKE US LOOK STUPID

BEING A CHRISTIAN WITHOUT BEING AN IDIOT!
11 ASSUMED TRUTHS THAT MAKE US LOOK STUPID

BRAD STINE

FIDELIS
BOOKS

A FIDELIS BOOKS BOOK
An Imprint of Post Hill Press
ISBN: 978-1-64293-525-7
ISBN (eBook): 978-1-64293-526-4

Being a Christian Without Being an Idiot!:
11 Assumed Truths That Make Us Look Stupid
© 2020 by Brad Stine
All Rights Reserved

Post Hill Press
New York • Nashville
posthillpress.com

Published in the United States of America

1 2 3 4 5 6 7 8 9 10

"Nothing matters but God."
— Brad Stine

CONTENTS

INTRODUCTION

Being a Christian Without Being an Idiot!

(The Rise of the Neo-Believer)

Hello, my fellow pilgrims, and welcome to my book.

The purpose of this book is to provoke thought, introspection, and even meditation on its ideas. Its contents may take many of you by surprise. I hope so, anyway, because if you saw this coming then you are a prophet and certainly in no need of my insight. Then again, if you were a prophet you wouldn't have had to buy this book in the first place, so I guess we can rule out that premise after all. But for you mere mortals I am not a theologian or intellectual—as anyone who has seen my show or watched me try to balance a checkbook can attest—nor am I a pastor, teacher, professor, or scholar. I am a comedian—a layman, a moron. I'm like you.

I am also a follower of Jesus Christ, which defines the very core of my life. Because I am a Conservative as well, most of my social/cultural dogma comes from that "ilk of thought." (I don't know if that's an actual coherent phrase, but it sounded clever and now that I'm an author I need as much cleverness as I can muster.) But if there is one thing I am sure of in my Christian walk, it's the fact there are many things in my walk

I'm not sure of. It was that simple but obvious revelation that jump-started this whole project. For instance, I always believed in the death penalty; yet, I am also an ardent pro-life advocate. I have performed for years at fundraisers for pregnancy resource centers and various pro-life events. One of the dynamics of many of these events was how ecumenical they were. There were often many Catholic priests attending even though the event was put on by Protestants. As a result, I found myself in conflict with many of my Catholic brethren, who were very much anti-death penalty.

As I explored this, I came to the realization the reason I was pro-death penalty was because I always assumed that's what the Bible taught. As I began to explore that notion, I found myself unable to discover exactly where this idea was located in the New Testament, which surprised me. You see, for me it was a foregone conclusion the death penalty was a "true" Christian position; only, I found that this position was a lot grayer than I realized. I took a personal stance on an extremely important position I assumed was true. That being said, while I still am in favor of the death penalty at this time (although the term "death penalty" sounds anti-Christian to my ears), I am now willing to examine my stance to see if it is biblically justified. Not only am I willing but as a true believer it is my DUTY!

From this experience, I realized how many believers are making moral and spiritual decisions based on Christian "truths" they assume to be true, when in reality they have become true based on a TRADITION of a particular denomination or group. This has often played out in my own life.

For instance, God uses me—and a very unorthodox communication scheme, comedy—to present a message. Even though I know this is my purpose, I have had to battle some Christians who felt my comedy style was distinctly "UN-Christian." It was in these moments I most realized how Satan will use this "Assumed Truth" (that is, what style a comedian who is also a Christian is supposed to have) to undermine the work of God through fellow believers, who demand all fellow followers march to their cadence.

It was because of my personal experiences I chose these eleven concepts to consider as a Christian. Are they really true or do we just believe them to be, even though there's no biblical support for them? More importantly, how does the belief in their veracity affect nonbelievers if we're wrong? Jesus said, "The truth shall set you free," which, by implication, must mean, "The false will imprison you." I, for one, am no longer willing to imprison the amazing grace and liberty my faith has given me to reach out to a world begging for authentic Christianity to save their terminally ill souls.

I have carefully considered these ideas as well as lived many of them. Some of you reading this may disagree with some of my conclusions, and that I don't mind, but if I have done nothing more than cause you to reevaluate what your faith means to you and in what shape it can come to you, then I have done my job. There is basically one overriding theme of this book and it's the fact Christians are different from each other in our theology, denominations, and social interaction, and you know what? That's AS IT SHOULD BE! The wider variety we come in, the more people we can reach! Christians on the "Assumed Truth" platform who historically have taken the position, "If you don't all behave exactly like me, then you're not really a Christian" have done, in my opinion, the greatest disservice to furthering the Gospel!

The groundwork for this book lies on that one presupposition.

I believe I'm where God wants me. After all, I couldn't do the work He's called me to do unless I'm where He wants me. He wants me on stage, and I believe this book was something God wanted me to write for a time such as this. God has decided to use the gift of comedy, which He gave me, to communicate to the unbelieving world, of that I am sure. It is my purpose. But I also believe God gave me an equally important message: to challenge fellow believers in the quality of their faith. Believe me, my friends, I don't take that lightly. And, trust me, not a day goes by when I don't recognize this message is perhaps more for me than you!

But, again, I'm like you, whether you like it or not. I am taking the liberty to write this book just as I do comedy—aggressively and unapologetically! I do that, not because I don't respect you, the reader, but because I do. If you're a Christian then we are brethren and FAMILY should be able to be the most honest with each other. We have no time for anything less.

We are at a place in our American history where the Christian worldview is mocked, ridiculed, and ignored. Though it is true there is a spiritual battle taking place with warriors who want to see this happen, I believe we have also brought much of this phenomenon on ourselves. This is not the time to be simply sweet and harmless and wonder why no one takes us seriously. The time of Stephen has passed. It's time to start wearing camel's hair coats, eating bugs, and tipping over tables! Not necessarily from a physical sense, mind you, but, and more importantly, from an intellectual place. It's time to take our beliefs seriously and start cleaning house, and that cleaning begins in our own house first!

It's hard to be human. It's harder yet being a Christian. It's really hard being a Christian in a world so antagonistic to the way you see the world. It's unbelievably hard being a Christian in a world that hates you while you're battling other Christians who are constantly judging your life, motives, and the sincerity of your walk!

So we need to take a second look at our attitudes toward other followers and our attitudes toward ideas that make nonbelievers think Christians are idiots. These are observations I've made over the years of things about us that make them turn and run—not toward Christ but away from Him. They are things many Christians believe are true— but they're not! So, that being said, you are going to have to prepare yourself in the way you read this book, since it's going to be a little different from others you have read from Christians.

I am a comedian and as such have written the book in a format I hope is humorous as well as thought-provoking. What you won't find are three verses to coincide with each statement I make. I have no particular training or credentials I can draw on in order to impress you. I am simply spewing forth my thoughts, concepts, and ideas, as if we were a couple of trusted friends talking together at lunch. Everything I know, or think I know, has come from two sources: (1) reading (the Bible and philosophical and apologetical literature) and (2) personal meditation (on God and ideas about Him). I asked trusted Christian associates to preview this book just to make sure there were no glaring heretical ideas promoted. If any heresy has skipped past these professionals, then I'm afraid it's their fault and they are the ones who are going to hell!

All kidding aside (like that's ever gonna happen!), all mature believers eventually come to realize they have a specific God-given purpose in life. I am coming to realize reluctantly that mine appears to be to rattle some cages and question paradigms. I didn't sign up for this assignment; it was given to me. I am literally called to be a missionary to America. Yet never in my entire life have I been afraid to be an unorthodox follower of Christ. Sure, I've taken some hits along the way, but that goes with the territory of being a Christian iconoclast. So I will just put on my thick skin and let the games begin!

SATAN SHOOTS HIMSELF IN THE HOOF

ASSUMED TRUTH 1: Satan causes most of the problems for Christians.

Catholics are all going to hell! At least, that was the kind of "open-minded insight" into the Christian realm I was taught growing up in a small Protestant church in the Midwest. They just couldn't reconcile how the idiosyncratic elements of some Catholics' faith could possibly allow them to be legitimate "born-again" Christians.

Yes, if self-righteousness were an art form, many Protestants' work would be in the Guggenheim! For some reason, ever since Protestants broke away from the Catholics, we have felt it our duty to explain how obsessive some Catholics are with elements of their faith. After all, there's nothing like a continuous family feud to make nonbelievers look upon us in envy, longing to be part of our "Good News."

Mary, for some reason, seems to be a major bone of contention with Protestants. Not that caring about Mary is necessarily idiosyncratic, it's just that to Protestants, she has never achieved dashboard status. Then again, to a Protestant, the ultimate place of status on a car isn't the dash anyways; it's the bumper. Whoever the guy was who designed the plastic fish accessory is no doubt living high on the hog somewhere in Malibu, eating really expensive actual fish. Of course, the plastic fish image to a Protestant has taken on the role of Mary to the Catholic, being a "must-have" symbol of our faith; yet, somehow, we don't consider it nearly as obsessive as theirs, fancy that!

No, we still feel it's our duty to find some flaw in the religious practices of our older sister, whom we divorced when Luther decided to announce to Christendom the emperor had no clothes. "Obsessive" really is the key word here. Why are there always certain people in every faith who have unique epiphanies that seem to pass the rest of us by? It's like the people who get abducted by aliens, not just once but numerous times! I have never even seen a UFO, let alone had the privilege of being "probed" by a higher life form.

Ironically, when you see these chosen few interviewed, you realize that if aliens chose THEM to study the human intellect, we as a species have been seriously underrepresented. Then again, if aliens are so smart, one would think they wouldn't choose those who have chosen to live in the desert in a trailer as the best representation of humanity. Of course, there are those Catholics who constantly witness the mystical in the most unlikely places, who give Protestants pause. For example, take the phenomenal way some Catholics seem to see Mary everywhere, her likeness periodically popping up in the most unholy places.

What's especially intriguing about Mary is how innovative she is. I mean, nothing is going to confirm your legitimacy as a religious icon more nobly than to suddenly display your image—on a tortilla! But, since I believe Christianity is truly the religion of reason, we should never fear examining any unprecedented occurrence.

For example, if this phenomenon is actually happening, I think there are two questions one must ask oneself: (1) logically speaking, since she's in heaven, how is she getting down here? and (2) why is she spending time projecting her likeness on somebody's screen door!? Not to mention if this phenomenon is possible, why aren't any of the other saints pulling it off, if for no other reason than to break the monotony of eternity? I mean, since Moses didn't even make it into the Promised Land, you'd think the least he could do is show up in a piece of toast somewhere in Sioux City, Iowa.

In any case, I hope when I become perfected in heaven, one of my many new abilities will be a wiser use of my time. I especially don't see me spending a lot of my time worrying about people down here. Sure, call me selfish, but when I finally get to heaven, I'm afraid you people are on your own! I mean, isn't that supposed to be one of the perks of heaven? We finally get to leave Earth?

If heaven is the ultimate place of perfection, what is it exactly I'm finding myself longing for down here, the climate? Of course, this brings up the question of IF departed saints are even ABLE to return to this much less appealing planet known as Earth. Does God really allow us to intervene in the land of the three-dimensional? If we could, don't you think we would do it with a little more flair than just a barely recognizable silhouette? I mean, people down here who haven't even reached perfected status yet are still able to slap together a few colors and brushstrokes, some of which have ended up on the Sistine Chapel. If a HUMAN can pull that off, I'm expecting a little more from the mother of GOD!

Now, wait before accusing me of Catholic "bashing." (By the way, the term "bashing" in the politically correct country we now find ourselves is generally a code word used by the true intellectual and ethical fascists of our society to authorize them to censor your point of view by associating your ideas with intolerance, bigotry, and racism without needing that annoying concept called evidence.)

I actually find many parts of Catholicism to be very intriguing, especially in the area of standing for absolute moral standards, as well as the passion for integrating the mystical elements of Christ in their mass. I think Protestants could use a lot more of the holy awe of God in our services; I know I could. The truth is, if you believe Jesus is God and is the only way to salvation, then guess what? You're a Christian! Let's battle our doctrinal differences in heaven!

For now Protestants and Catholics need each other as a united front against the real enemy of secular humanism! Every religion is fraught with the fringe or fanatical crowd who in their zeal to prove their allegiance always end up being embarrassing to the rest of us. Catholics aren't exactly alone with these visionary appearances. Sure, some Catholics may see Mary everywhere, but some Protestants see SATAN everywhere! There is even a Christian television channel providing training so you can see Satan's unique handiwork. You've heard 'em: "Help! Satan's in my computer! Satan's in my radio! Satan cost me my job!"

I have a thought. Maybe your incompetence cost you your job!

First of all, where in the New Testament do we see Satan ever possessing someone and then being cast out?

For those of you who find research a tad too labor-intensive, I'll tell you.

NEVER!! We see demons cast out of people, but Satan's nowhere to be found.

Apparently, afflicting people with leprosy is beneath him. There is something about those oozing sores that are frankly a bit yucky even for Satan. Again, the first time we see Satan in the New Testament is when he appears to Jesus in a misguided attempt to seduce Him.

Gee, isn't this the same guy who, while living in the presence of God, decided he could claim equal authority with Him, thus getting his hind end thrown out of paradise? Then, when God comes to Earth he tries the same thing. This is the mental giant with whom we are doing daily battle?

Not that I doubt Satan has real power. Anyone who has experienced serious pain in life knows just how evil Satan can be. I mean, pain exists because Satan exists. But remember, he fell first! Satan made the decision to tell God He was no longer necessary, thus bringing the need for God to judge him. Judgment comes to those who disobey the perfect standards God put into place. The punishment for disobedience is always painful.

Then Satan, being evil, decided if he was going to burn, he was taking others with him. He tempts Adam and Eve, who fall, thus ending the perfect fellowship they had with their Creator and marking the beginning of pain and the need for a wardrobe, which apparently is the one upside women found in the Fall. Yeah, we're gonna die but we get to wear ninety different pairs of shoes over our lifetime to get there!

So, in observation, much of our pain apparently is a result of the behavioral choices stemming from the heart. Even death, the ultimate triumph of evil, came as a result of our choice to disobey God. In other words, humans were not designed to die—we just figured out how to do it!

A follower's relationship with and response to Satan is pretty well spelled out in the Gospel. We first see Satan in the New Testament trying his hand at tempting Christ to sin.

Notice Satan is tempting, not possessing! Why? First, you don't send a demon to do a devil's job. He was going after God in the flesh. He knew he couldn't fool Jesus about his involvement in this escapade, so he didn't even try. He is just arrogant enough to think he could pull it off.

But notice something closely: nowhere do we see Jesus battling Satan's overwhelming supernatural power. There is no lightning being called down from heaven, no screaming demons clawing at his clothes, not even the arbitrary locust. Instead, we see Satan attempting to trip Jesus up by creating the opportunity for Jesus to decide to destroy Himself.

Satan's "style" (and I use that term loosely) hasn't changed since the beginning. He approached Jesus on three human appetites. Let's examine a couple to see what he was up to. First, he appealed to his physical needs: "Make these stones become bread." Now, this was a legitimate test. Jesus was hungry, and hunger is good. Jesus had an actual physical need. His body needed nourishment.

Forty days without food would leave anyone a little famished, except maybe a supermodel as long as she had a pack of Marlboro's.

Satan says, "If you are the Son of God, tell this stone to become bread." Where exactly is the temptation here? Jesus IS hungry. Jesus DOES want to eat. Jesus COULD turn stones to bread, and best of all, Jesus IS the Son of God!

It seems as if Satan is really dealing with subtlety here.

What kind of a statement is that—"If you are the Son of God"? It's almost as if had Jesus done this simple miracle ("simple miracle" makes about as much sense as a "giant dwarf"), He would have in effect been trying to prove something to Satan. Satan knew exactly who Jesus was, yet he tried to get Him to jump through hoops as though He owed Satan something.

This is the same reasoning people today use to not believe. If God is real, He has to heal my wife, get me out of this debt, and so on. God is under no obligation to do anything to or for us to prove anything! WE DO NOT DICTATE TO OUR CREATOR THE MEANS BY WHICH HE MUST VALIDATE HIMSELF TO US!! Yet equally important is the fact we don't necessarily know what we need during trials.

We would choose bread if we were hungry yet Jesus makes it clear what my body desires is irrelevant; I will wait until the Lord provides for me what I actually need. You see, this is a constant inconsistency with atheists. They don't believe in God because there is evil in the world. Gee, by that logic, wouldn't it mean God must exist because there is GOOD in the world?

The biggest problem with atheists is they believe in God only if He behaves in the manner they have defined for Him, but in order for Him to be God, He would have to behave differently than any of us could truly grasp. I'll talk about this more in depth (and then some!) later.

God does it the way HE chooses, in HIS time, and in HIS way. The minute we are able to define the means by which God must behave, He has become subject to our whims and is no longer the omnipotent One. No matter how difficult it becomes for us to accept the ways God chooses to intervene in our lives at times, the maturity of a follower is shown in the understanding our sense of how this particular scenario should play out is irrelevant.

We also see Jesus answered Satan with the phrase, "Man does not live on bread alone." This is in reference to the manna from heaven God provided to the children of Israel. Jesus knew His Father would provide for Him in ways even He might not fully comprehend or anticipate. Of course, it might seem that being fully God AND man would mean that there is nothing He wouldn't know. But wouldn't it be better if there were times He relinquished some of His omniscience so as to be able to rightly say, "I know exactly what you're struggling with, I've been there"? Jesus was willing and able to wait for God's timing. He, unlike us, never felt the need to hurry God. He knew He would always get whatever He needed whenever He needed it: the key word here being "needed"— not "wanted."

The follower can't have a fast-food mentality when it comes to the things of God. Once again, the curse of the Western Christian has taught us that to wait for God's answer is a burden, not, as it should be seen, a relief. Jesus knew even the thing that is good for us is only good in God's time.

The second temptation was when Satan took Christ to the top of a building and declared, "Throw yourself off for it says in Scripture, 'He will send angels to protect thee lest you bash your foot upon a stone.' " Jesus answered with the Word, "It is also written thou shall not tempt the Lord thy God." Interestingly, this foreshadows what Jesus would instruct his followers to include in the prayers they offer to the Father. The Lord's Prayer literally says, "Lead us not into temptation, but deliver us from evil." I wonder if there might be the idea that God is not in the business of putting on a show. His powers of intervention in our lives are not designed to be a spectacle.

Actually, during Jesus's ministry he informed the freshly healed person to not tell anyone what had just happened. He could inform the priest in order to confirm God is here and moving but Jesus wasn't seeking an audience by which he could have crowds of people swooning over his physical manifestations of God's work, all the while waving his cloak around to "slay people in the spirit," causing them to losing control of their faculties and faint as they hit the ground. Interestingly, when this alleged phenomenon is put on display, you will fortuitously discover the church has provided "catchers" to keep the person from bumping their head as they collapse as well as drape a cloth across a woman's legs to protect her modesty.

So let me get this straight. God is going to knock people out but doesn't anticipate they could get injured on the way down and their lying there could also cause some men to stumble with the temptation of lust in examining a woman's exposed legs. So either God didn't think this through or a spectacle was exactly what the Lord wasn't in the business of manufacturing. I'm guessing if God Almighty chose to engage in some form of communal outpouring of His spirit, which He is entirely free to do if He chooses, it wouldn't look like a poor man's version of a hypnosis show. But maybe that's just me?

Human challenges and trials are our daily spiritual workout to practice new behavior and to rehearse how we instantly respond to adversity, the one and only way we will ever learn how to renew our minds. As followers, we need to review our perception of trials. They are not purposeless burdens but the necessary means God has chosen to give us the opportunity to serve Him.

This is why we can thank God when trials come our way because, when we see them as God trusting us to respond with His likeness, He is honoring us by His confidence in our maturity. Of course, who needs that kind of pressure? It's easier to find a scapegoat to our un-Christ-like responses. The concept that demons are at the root of all our problems is the Christian's journey into the wonderful world of "not my responsibility." This idea has become so ingrained in the new American psyche, a destination so often traveled to, it should become our fifty-first state! Welcome, visitors, to the state of "It's Not My Fault," and please, before you leave, don't forget to tour the capital city of "Blame Others for My Dysfunction."

We are Americans, for goodness sake. We think trials are when we can only afford one car. Tribulations are not being able to pray publicly before a football game. Wake up! Try being a Christian in North Korea or the Middle East. They have discovered the true meaning of being a follower. We pray for them because many are thrown in prison, many are enslaved, many are killed. Yet they continue to grow in faith and in numbers! See, that's the secret: finding that nothing in your life matters more than Christ. Not comfort, not riches, nothing.

When you become a Christian in China, you know exactly what the price is. If you are a follower in Sudan, you know exactly the cost you are going to be asked to pay. What is it exactly they experience we haven't thus far? (You're not going to want to hear this....) PERSECUTION! We pray for them over here, as well we should, that they will be freed from their prisons and released from their tormentors, yet we are missing the point.

WE ARE ALSO IN PRISON! The prison of consumer goods: we are enslaved to our comforts and desires. We look at the riches of this country and believe we must be blessed from God. Yet, Jesus was very specific in who would have the hardest time reaching heaven. NOT the persecuted, not even those who never heard His name. No, it is the RICH who will have the most difficult time making it!!

Who lives in the richest nation on Earth? We do! Unless you are actually gnashing your teeth, foaming at the mouth, and being thrown into the occasional campfire, I don't think Satan is the biggest obstacle in your life!

Don't get me wrong. Satan is real. Jesus said so. But Satan's true strength is deception. I mean, look at Adam and Eve in the garden. When we read this story, nowhere do we see God warning them about Satan. I mean, they didn't even know of his existence! Their only warning was from God: "Do not eat of this tree." God put the responsibility on them. He knew Satan was there. He even knew he was going to try to deceive them. Yet God only focused on one thing: "Are you going to obey me?" No excuses!

Again, it's as if Satan's only role is to provide the opportunity for us to disobey. We do the choosing. Of course, it's important to be aware of Satan's work in the world and especially in our own lives. But just as our definition of who

God is colors how we worship Him, the same can be said for a healthy or unhealthy way of viewing Satan.

The bottom line is Satan is real, but he's overrated. I mean, look at the powers we ascribe to him. We consider him to be the ultimate evil guy. No one is more wicked or devious, and yet, no one has ever actually seen him! But we've all seen pictures and if you've seen a picture of Satan, you can see why he's lying low!

I mean, if your job was to be the ultimate scourge on humanity, sneaking around among us without detection, wouldn't you have chosen a less obvious costume by now?! Seems to me, if you're trying to be inconspicuous, maybe you shouldn't be completely RED, for example! Maybe you should stop carrying a pitchfork for no apparent reason, and, for crying out loud, Satan, put on some pants! In every picture of Satan, he's never wearing pants! Just how intimidating can a pantless red guy be!?

Even worse, while some Christians are always looking for the latest place Satan means to rear his horny head, they never see it as a spiritual battle involving obedience. If they have a problem with something in our culture, the response seems to be threefold. First, to fear it, then condemn it, and then try to ban it!! Tell me, when in our history did banning anything ever result in a positive outcome? I mean, we banned alcohol once. Boy, did that work like a charm!

Yeah, you couldn't find a drink at all in the Roaring Twenties!! Just ask Al Capone!

Nope, they just keep trying to ban stuff. Just look at the people who want to ban guns. I'm not saying we shouldn't look at or consider problems of violence in our society, but what bothers me is some think banning something will make the specific problem go away. The problem is never the object to be banned; it's always the problem of the human heart!

Banning is a cover for the fact the secular mind cannot find solutions to society's problems and doesn't know what to do about it. It's so pathetically simplistic, it's laughable. Let me get this straight: ban guns and suddenly everyone will be nice to each other?! If banning is that effective, why not just cut to the chase? I know, let's ban crime!! Sure, I can see the crooks now: "Well, I was going to shoot that guy, but apparently it's 'illegal' now. Guess I'll have to turn to a life of labor." Here, let me take a moment to spoon-feed a little common sense to any progressive ideologues who may accidentally be reading this book.

Guns don't kill people—bullets kill people! If there is a bullet in a gun, someone put it there. If someone put it there, he did it on purpose. If he did it on purpose, it means he made a choice. If he made a choice, it's because he has reason. If he has reason, it means he's autonomous. If he's autonomous, it means he can choose between right and wrong. If he pointed the gun at someone and pulled the trigger, it means he meant to! If he meant to, that means he knew what he was doing and what would happen after he did. It's HIS fault! That is so obvious, it would take an "intellectual" like a tenured professor from Berkeley to be unable to follow the logic.

Notice how our secular society has begun to mirror the original sin in that everyone who committed sin in the garden blamed someone else! Sound familiar? The only one who had the guts to take responsibility for his actions was SATAN! He enjoys watching us in pain and like a serial arsonist, he loves to watch his handiwork burn!

You see, a believer is always sensitive to what is going to be the most effective way to represent Christ. Take, for instance, the entire flap over the *Harry Potter* books a while back, with the claims they were teaching kids about sorcery and magic, and the like. I'm not even going to comment on the fact the greatest Christian apologist of the twentieth century, C. S. Lewis, used these same concepts to create the *Narnia* books. (Actually, I guess I did just comment on it!)

I wonder if the churches in New Mexico and Ohio took that into consideration when they had their *Harry Potter* book-burning extravaganzas. They engaged in book burning, for crying out loud. Gee, I wonder why that hasn't caught on with more churches, considering all the nonbelievers who flocked to their doors after this paranoid display. Nothing I can think of is more productive in bringing nonbelievers through the church door than a good old-fashioned book burning!

You know, next time you consider this method, you need to really think it through a bit. Any methodology Christians use to present their belief system to the world is supposed to draw people to the cross, not send them fleeing in horror. I think a good rule of thumb is, if HITLER tried it, you may want to go another direction! The fear of some Christians that their kids are going to be negatively impacted by elements of our culture actually is a higher indictment of the fact so few parents are able or willing to take the time to teach their kids about the Christian worldview.

How about this for an option? Read *Harry Potter* with your kids and afterward discuss the difference between what this story means and what we as followers of Jesus believe! This way, when our kids go to school, where everyone they know has read the books, they will be able to articulate their worldview rationally and intelligently. What a concept. Oh, well, just call me a dreamer.

Although that would have sure helped me when I was growing up. When I was a kid, I was taught that one of Satan's most evil tricks was—are you ready?!—BACKWARD MASKING!!! If you don't know what that is, it's the belief there were messages in rock and roll records you could only hear if they were played backward!

Just how do you expect anyone else to take your faith seriously, when you are serious about this nonsense? Let's try something innovative and use our minds for a second.

Simply put yourself in a nonbeliever's shoes. First, you hear about this great faith of love and compassion, then you hear, "Yes, if you take certain rock and roll records and you play them backward..."—as so many of us tend to do?

I'm sorry, but if you're starting to play your records backward, perhaps you deserve to hear a message from Satan! He's probably just giving instructions: "IT'S GOING THE WRONG WAY! CAN I BORROW YOUR PANTS?!"

Who came up with this concept anyway, this idea that my subconscious is able to decipher phrases placed backward in a record I'm listening to forward!? Have you listened to any rock and roll from the seventies? It's pretty much next to impossible to figure out what they're saying even when you play it the right way!

Look, if backward words were evil, then all words backward could be potentially dangerous tools of Satan! For example, Dallas, Texas. People in Dallas would start becoming possessed by eating cabbage. Why? Because "Dallas" backward is "salad"!

I have firsthand experience with the ignorance of Christians who "mean well," but who end up just being, well, mean. Since the age of thirteen I have indulged in the hobby of performing magic tricks (oops, I just lost my Baptist readers)—I mean illusions (there go the Charismatics)—okay, okay, I was a performer of sleight of hand or what's referred to nowadays as street magic.

My first professional gig was at a restaurant in Bremen, Indiana, where I lived at the time. I put cards on the table of this restaurant in the heart of a Conservative farming community, telling the patrons that for three dollars, they could request my services. Since nobody had three dollars in that town (why else come to the $2.98 buffet?), I usually ended up going around to the tables and asking if they would like to see some magic tricks.

One evening a couple from my church whom I respected came in. Being a naive eighteen-year-old, I figured they would get a kick out of my repertoire. I approached the table, and, in my most humble yet proud voice, asked them if they would like to see some of my magic tricks. I'll never forget the response I got from this good Christian woman.

"Well, you know, Brad, magic is of the devil."

Forget the disappointment, embarrassment, and hurt feelings; there was also that great philosophical debate within my mind the great theologians have wrestled with from the beginning of the Church. How do we stop Satan from his insidious attacks on this earth using that most diabolical and ruthless of schemes—the card trick!?

I can't begin to count the number of souls burning in hell today because they so foolishly and recklessly had some guy find their ace of spades buried in a "perfectly ordinary deck of cards," or watched in pleasure as one coin "evilly" disappeared from one hand and reappeared in the other.

Are there Christians who actually believe Satan, as vain as he is, would try to draw them into his grasp with such trivialities? No, I think his real trick is fairly obvious. Plant the seed in the mind of the typical fundamentalist that sleight-of-hand magic tricks are evil. Have the same person make a big deal about this in front of somebody, preferably a nonbeliever. Then stand back and watch the fun as this nonbeliever, confused by this irrationality, walks away shaking his head, pondering what he has expected all along: Christians are misguided, uneducated, backward, ignorant fools.

I believe the follower's number one purpose in life is to demonstrate reasonably, authentically, and lovingly the Truth, which is Jesus. It's a little difficult to do this when we act like idiots to the rest of the world.

This is where Satan's skills truly come into play. Allow the Christians to destroy their own credibility by being intellectually, well, un-credible. Satan barely lifts a hoof and voilà! Another soul bound for the kingdom of hell.

My friends, before I became a comedian I made a living as a professional sleight-of-hand artist for a number of years. Some of the best in the world are friends of mine. I'm going to give you a special spiritual phrase you need to pass on to the next Christian you find embarrassing the rest of us with their misunderstanding of the art of illusion. Gently, yet firmly, in love of course, scream as loud as possible, "IT'S JUST A CARD TRICK!!"

DEAD PEOPLE ALWAYS RUN LATE

ASSUMED TRUTH 2: Christians
shouldn't hurt over death.

I can't stand being late! I'm one of those people who will get
to an event thirty minutes early, then hide down the street
until it's time to arrive. Consequently, people who are late
drive me crazy, especially the chronically late! They bug me
because they act like it's not their fault, like it's encoded in
their genes. They seem to think no one is inconvenienced and
we all actually find them to be quirky and quaint. (By the way,
not everyone can use two of the twelve existing "Q" words in
one sentence! I'm good!) So they never act contrite.

That's all I'm really asking from the late person—
contrition. Something simple like, "I am so sorry, what can
I do to repay you?" Then we would have actual punishment:
"You must stand in line for me at the DMV, and call me
when it's my turn," and the like. But the only people who
are sorry for being late are those of us who rarely are! The
chronic "lateaholics" are never sorry! Worse yet, they think it's
funny! They always come bounding in, completely unaware

of the time. Why do they even wear watches, since apparently time isn't a set standard of measurement for them? It's only a suggestion! They see time as their enemy, and they take it personally! That's why they say they're "killing time"! They're like the Mafia: they want it dead! They don't live by the same parameters as the rest of us. They never understand the concept of "three o'clock"; they live in the world of "around three" or "three-ISH," and the classic "between the hours of eight and five," a parameter usually reserved for the likes of exterminators and plumbers.

Can you imagine living in a world that gives you a nine-hour window as to when you might show up? Then no matter how irresponsible you are that day, when you decide to roll into town, you are actually on time! Of course, those who haven't created this boundaryless ETA like to rub salt in the wound—they try to deflect any responsibility for their lateness by instantly spouting their favorite phrase, "I'm running late" (always accompanied by a silly aw-shucks laugh and grin), followed by some pithy statement like, "It's the story of my life—ha, ha, ha."

And they always use verbs to describe their behavior that never reflect what's really going on, as in the term "running late." First problem: What does the term "running late" even mean? It's an oxymoron! How can you be running and late at the same time?! It sounds like you are going to be late—as fast as you can? If you were running, you should have made it! Others try the phrase "running behind." Running behind who, ME!!? And I'm not even moving! You know why? I'm waiting for you!

It drives me nuts! But, if you're a Christian, you constantly have to walk that fine line between forgiveness/non-judgment and holding someone accountable/righteous indignation. I mean, no matter how rude, inconvenienced, and angry we are, what is the phrase we always hear spilling out of our mouths?

"No problem."

No problem?! How can it not be a problem? Yes, I envision a utopian world where people decide to show up at any arbitrary time, without regard for the rest of us! Of course, some jobs probably function better when they are on time. Nothing specific comes to mind, but—oh, say, perhaps firemen would fit that category, and bus drivers, and, of course, the catchers in a flying trapeze act. Yes, if they show up late, I'm thinking that lands in the "problem" category. Otherwise, what's the word "problem" for just math?

I think that's the word we should use more often: problem! They come dancing in, saying, "I'm running late, ha, ha, ha, story of my life," then we say, "Problem!" YES! PROBLEM!! Why are we so afraid to tell late people they're late? I'll tell you why. Because we don't want to hurt their feelings. Nowadays, the need to avoid hurting someone's feelings is more important than anything else we do, including the expectation of common sense and personal responsibility. Offending someone is the progressives' worst nightmare; they're driven by its implications. Of course, everyone else suffers for their commitment to it. If "tolerance" is the progressives' God, "censoring dissent" is their hatchet man.

As a matter of fact, the only people we will accuse of being late, and tell them to their faces, are dead people! We'll say "the late Fred Girard," or "the late Ethel Slaso." Yeah, they are late. You know why? THEY'RE DEAD!! Not only are they late, but I think it's a safe bet they're not going to show up at all!

Death is one of the great paradoxes of humanity; we know it's the one stage of existence onto which everyone must enter. No one is exempt. Everyone goes, rich and poor, movie stars and homeless, Dick Clark and Methuselah. We all take this journey. We all know we are going to die, yet somehow, we really don't believe it! Why else would people ask, when given the news of their impending demise, "Why is this happening to me?" This demonstrates the delusional world we continue to inhabit.

I could understand the phrase, "Why NOW?" but never just, "Why?" Every human has one thing in common: we are all terminally ill! The moment we're conceived, we are at the front edge of the journey we know as "life." If it ran according to our own plan, we would live with two stable, loving parents. We would get through school relatively unscathed and acquire some sort of degree. We would marry the person of our dreams and have wonderful, well-behaved children. We'd have a completely fulfilling job making more money than we ever imagined. We would live a healthy, full life, spending the holidays with the kids and grandkids at our side. We would retire with our spouse and travel extensively, and, finally, at a ripe old age, at the final outer edge of our life, as all our lineage stands around our bed, we would utter some last immortal words of wisdom that will inspire generations to come, only to painlessly and without fear or effort depart this mortal coil, leaving a legacy all will honor. But notice, even under this most unlikely and rare scenario, the end of the story is still YOU'RE DEAD!! Where is the happy ending?

Even in the movies, we can't conceive of eternal life on Earth in a positive light. The only people you see who never die are monsters! Zombies, some kind of otherworldly thing, even though their clothes are tattered and most of their flesh has been removed, have still acquired superhuman strength! They can only walk one mile an hour, but if they happen to catch you, which is usually as a result of a twisted ankle or a car that won't start, they are able to lift you over their heads and throw you twenty feet in the air.

What exactly are monsters so angry about anyway? Just how tough can their life be? In my opinion, they've got it made! Think of all the upsides to being a monster.

One thing that springs to mind is no fear of the dark. I remember as a kid longing for the day when I got to be old enough to walk into a dark house alone at night and not feel that clammy death hand about to grab the back of my neck (I'm still waiting). Monsters, on the other hand, are not afraid of anything really. I mean, you don't fear death if you're already dead. They don't have bills to pay and aren't concerned with fashion trends; they pretty much wear the same tattered outfit every day. Still, it could get lonely if every time you try to talk with someone, they flee in terror. I mean, I don't want to be accused of profiling or anything, but if you're a monster and try to infiltrate the living human's domain, you're probably not going to blend in.

Something about the hanging eyeball and missing skullcap is usually a dead giveaway.

But I don't blame you for trying to make friends with the living. It would make life a lot easier for you and give us, Christians in particular, a chance to practice our altruism. Hey, if you need something, let us get it for you. We'll probably have better luck since we can go shopping in the daytime. You know, when stores are open. We won't have to smash our arms through the windows or anything! Just another one of the many perks for those of us not in the final stages of putrefaction.

Anyway, the point is: How are we to think about death? I mean, if a follower of Jesus is unable to demonstrate hope and meaning regarding this most disturbing and frightening element of the human experience, what exactly is our religion for? But that's exactly what the Bible tells us about death!

After all, it gives us instances of two different—and significant—people reacting to the experience of death. First, there's Paul, who wanted nothing from his life but to share Christ; yet he longed to die. "To live is Christ, to die is gain!" Paul saw great hope in death.

But wait a minute! Aren't we supposed to be living a life of joy on Earth indescribably superior to our fellow humans? Didn't Jesus say He came to bring life and that more abundantly?! I mean, have you ever known people in your circle of relationships who truly, unequivocally, absolutely loved life? No matter what circumstances came their way they seemed happy. They spent every moment, from sunrise to sunset, truly enjoying the day.

We've all known the kind of person who always had a kind word for everyone, whose countenance seemed to shine. Someone you could tell had honestly found true contentment and peace. The kind of person who, as you watched day in and day out looking for some chink in the armor, just seemed to get healthier and more assured of themselves until you finally just wanted to puke?!

These people do exist and their existence is just another beacon along the road of life, reminding the rest of us exactly where we're never going to arrive. Yet no matter how advanced we are in our spiritual walk we all have some degree of apprehension about death. That's natural!

Human nature!

Oh, sure, you can play the American Christian game of assuring all of us how you long to enter into the Kingdom of God, and I'm sure you do! We all do!! But the truth is most of us are going to get there by dying, and dying is spooky. It's supposed to be, considering death was the first punishment for man's first sin. Death is unnatural. Our bodies weren't designed to die and, considering your body does all the dying (our spirit takes it from there), it hangs on with everything it's got. It fears its annihilation and wants no part of it.

For the true believer, death should be painful because it's a reminder of our separation from our Creator. It also forces our loved ones to be separated from us for a time. (Why is it, by the way, we all generally hold ourselves in such a position of esteem we can't imagine how our loved ones could possibly get along without us?) Yes, death has been defeated, but the remnant of its vicious assault on humanity continues.

Authentic Christianity hates death. It doesn't try to gloss over its pain in some pathetic illusory world we have created, trying to show our fellow humans how "strong" and unaffected we are. Authentic Christianity weeps with the brokenhearted and curses the evil sin has given us.

Authentic believers should be the most in touch with all the expressions of emotion God has given us, including grief. Christians are supposed to change the world but behaving as though pain doesn't exist changes no one because it's a lie.

Think about it. What is going to encourage a nonbeliever most in the midst of tragedy? The Christian who "encourages" them with what has to be the most inappropriate phrase ever to be uttered in front of a child's casket, "He's in a better place," or the equally insensitive "It's God's will"? Truth is truth, but when it's not distributed with a discretion designed to heal, it comes across exactly as it is, insensitive and, frankly, stupid!

Where and when exactly did we formulate the concept believers are supposed to pretend we are oblivious to the pain of death? Not from the Bible! That's not what Jesus shows us about death.

Look at the story of Lazarus. Remember when Jesus first heard the news that Lazarus was sick? He knew Lazarus would eventually die. He even hung around a little longer to make sure it took place. He even told His disciples Lazarus was dead. When they went to the tomb, Jesus KNEW He was going to raise his friend from the dead; He even said that was why He let him die! So, now, follow me here:

Jesus knew Lazarus was dying. Jesus let him die.

Jesus knew He was going to raise him from the dead.

Why the recap, you ask? Because when Jesus arrived at the tomb to perform this miracle that would bring awe and unspeakable joy to the family of the deceased—a miraculous act that would show all those present Jesus had power over death—Jesus observed the grieving around Him, all the while knowing in only moments they were going to receive an answered prayer that millions of grieving families have prayed from the beginning of time.

Even knowing all that—this God/man cried. We must ask why. Why cry for a dead man you know in thirty seconds is about to be very much alive, though I'm sure also very confused?

The Bible observes something about this moment, and I think it is the obvious answer. It says, as Jesus saw Mary weeping and all the others weeping with her, He was moved to deep compassion and joined her in her sorrow.

Not only did He demonstrate the importance of joining others in grief but He acknowledged the death experience as something to detest. He acknowledged her pain and didn't offer any trite "Christianese" phrases to try and alter her emotions. Even believers who are aware their ultimate destiny in death is heaven can learn from Jesus's response to the soon-to-be-living Lazarus. There is still a legitimate element of sorrow in the experience.

This three-dimensional life we live is the beginning edge of eternity for our existence. Yet it is the only time in our eternal existence when pain is the norm. Shakespeare said, "All the world's a stage, and we are just players on it." Yet this play is an endless loop echoing the first performance. The characters change, but our "character" doesn't. It's the same tired formula.

We traded eternal intimacy with the Creator for the desire to be Him. The pain and havoc that decision has played out on the human stage has never ended. The play we are in is a drama, and it always ends the same. We die. We still believe it's unfair. We continue to utilize our severely limited capacity of reason to find fault with God over this issue without full knowledge of the facts. We somehow believe we should be exempt from consequences we brought on ourselves. Justice never seems to enter the equation—or at least a justice that makes sense to us! Hell is an extreme punishment that doesn't fit the crime.

Nobody ever thinks they deserve eternal punishment, but you never have any problem persuading someone they can have eternal paradise. We may not understand heaven, we may even go as far as to say we don't really deserve it, but when God offers it anyway, we receive it with the awareness of just how good God can be. Here we have the Rule Maker. This is the One who put order into disorder; the One who was very specific about the wages of sin.

When Satan rebelled, God created the punishment He said was deserving of this treason. Then, when man rebelled again and again, knowing full well the punishment already in place for this action, God didn't quit on us. Satan wasn't apparently even given a chance to repent.

WE WERE! God didn't say to us, "Oh, well, you were warned, to hell with you then." Instead, He said, "Don't worry, kids, I'm coming down there!" He sacrificed a piece of His essence to demonstrate to what lengths God is willing to stoop in order to hold you in His care. God's sacrifice defies logic. He transformed into the very kind of being He created us to be. He then allowed this "intelligent dirt" to ridicule Him, hate Him, kill Him, and even deny He IS!

Think of this irony: His power alone allows us to exist, so some of us can use our existence to deny His! For God, then, to pay for the sins of such a pathetic creature and still allow him the "right" to choose to despise Him is beyond my ability to comprehend. God's patience is miraculous.

When I consider how angry I get from something as unimportant as someone cutting in front of me without using a turn signal or being late for an appointment, it's obvious why God didn't give humans omnipotence. You thought the God of the Old Testament was harsh? Ha! Just give me the ability to call locusts from heaven every time I perceive I have been wronged, and nobody would be left on Earth but me. (Oh, what the heck, I suppose I would keep my wife too.)

God has to be patient, I suppose, considering He gave us that double-edged sword known as choice. Even human parents are very aware that some of the most difficult moments of parenting involve allowing a child to make a choice we know is going to harm them, simply so we can teach them they are ultimately responsible for their own actions. Imagine the pain of allowing someone to choose hell because you refuse to force someone into an inauthentic relationship with you.

Yes, this is the real issue with death, isn't it? It's bad enough to cease to exist, but to spend eternity in damnation is the one area humans refuse to accept. This is one area for which God is constantly getting a bad rap. Yet there is a huge difference between the idea God "throws people into hell" and He lets them choose hell.

The hell concept is one of the most difficult elements of God we humans can ever meditate on. The truth is we as humans simply do not want to have to pay for our choices. God was very specific about the fact that hell does exist and it is the punishment for disobedience. It wasn't meant for humans and He did provide a way out of it. We just want the ability to do as we choose without consequences! Well, I'm afraid, folks, that just ain't gonna happen. Gravity is still gravity whether we believe in it or not and there are plenty of tall edifices around if you ever want to prove it pragmatically. If the Creator exists, then, by definition, He makes the rules. You don't have to like the rules; nevertheless, you're governed by them.

Wanting to deny our responsibility is the same immature mentality that sparks anger in us when a policeman hides in the bushes to catch a driver speeding. We don't want him to hide because we want the chance to slow down so we can appear to be obeying the law instead of actually doing it. When we are caught we act as if the person put in charge of upholding the law did something wrong. In our minds, tickets are supposed to be given out to the real jerks on the highway. If you're not sure who the real jerks are, they're easy to spot. They are always the people who aren't us!

Rules are always meant for the other guy. I once heard the late Ed Cole, the author of *Maximized Manhood*, say in a sermon, "We as humans tend to judge others by what they do; we judge ourselves by our intentions." A "No Parking" sign, for example, actually means you can park there as long as you're sitting at the wheel with the motor running. Apparently, there is a difference between parking and waiting. A handicapped zone is for handicapped people only, except, of course, if you're "just running in for a second."

God hates hell and He hates when any of His creation choose to go there. But don't blame God for being consistent to His character. He demands a price for sin. "The wages of sin are death." He has also provided the means to escape it. How can anyone possibly hold God responsible for being "unfair," when He explicitly laid out the rules?

You want more grace? Every moment we exist on this earth is grace! Every time we are given the message of hope that Jesus died for us, we are given grace. If you have heard the means by which God has provided your escape, and then choose to disregard them, you have no one to blame but yourself.

God finds no pleasure in punishment any more than we parents on Earth do. But to demand our "right" to enter His kingdom on our terms is such an insult to the price paid on our behalf that I'm more amazed He isn't happy some of us go to hell. But that is the true nature of God. God is love. There is no "monster" in heaven who finds great glee in throwing someone into the midst of eternal damnation. There is, instead, a Creator so benevolent He watches in pain and horror as one of His beloved creations walks into the midst of a fiery destiny they were never designed to endure. And just think—they will be eternally, fully conscious of the fact they are fulfilling the life they so arrogantly chose.

But for me, I have chosen another destiny. Someday I am going to die. As a Christ follower, I believe my spirit will leave this body and unite with my Creator. I will enter the domain formally reserved for the Almighty. I will probably spend the first four or five millennia on my face trying to work up the courage to look into the eyes or light or whatever essence God actually inhabits. I will be in the midst of joy unspeakable! I will finally be free from pain and from fear. I will have victory over the anger and bitterness that have ruled my life since I can remember. I will finally be able to represent my Savior in a fashion worthy of Him, because, of course, finally, I will be like Him!

Of course, it's possible this is all an illusion. A true follower of Christ can't "know" any of this is true. Only that we believe it to be. The world of God is outside the five senses that on Earth we use as a gauge to determine the reality of anything material. To pretend it isn't is not authentic behavior to the nonbeliever. I believe what I believe can withstand intellectual scrutiny. Any belief system that can't withstand intellectual scrutiny is not worthy of my allegiance. We'll discuss this later. But I leave you with this thought. If atheists are right and there is no hereafter, only eternal unconsciousness, the sad conclusion is they'll never know! Of course, if they're wrong, they'll know forever.

That, to paraphrase Pascal, is a gamble no rational person should take.

BE NOT DRUNK WITH GRAPE JUICE

ASSUMED TRUTH 3: Drinking
and smoking are sins.

Humans are obsessed with their looks. In every culture and in every tribe, from the heart of New York City to the most remote village on Earth, no matter how harsh the environment or how technologically advanced we are, the one thing we all have in common is that we have a face! And if we have a face, one thing for sure is someone else is probably looking at it. And if it's being looked at, we want it to look good! Not just good, but better-looking than another face you might happen to come across. In order to accomplish this crucial task, humans have always made it a practice to do something, anything, to draw attention to themselves.

In the beginning, it was a much simpler life. Look at Adam and Eve. They didn't wear the hottest trend in clothes because they didn't wear clothes at all! They weren't caught up with this obsession to appear hip. No tailored suits, no highlighted hair. No makeup, no high heels, no sexy lingerie. No, they just went with your basic naked.

A decision, I might add, that works fine with me. You give me a choice between a woman in the hottest fashion, the latest coiffeur, and the trendiest eye shadow, and a woman in basic nude, I'm pretty much going that direction. After all, I'm a guy. I'm a Christian guy, but I have a news flash for those of you who aren't aware: Christian men prefer naked as well as the next guy. To say anything different would be inauthentic, which, as you know, is not the purpose of this book.

Naked is good!! It has to be; God invented it! The only differentiation between a pagan and me is the context.

Everything I choose must be in context with the way God made the rules. That's why it was good in Eden; it was in the context of God's will. This was a husband and wife alone in paradise. Well, not completely alone—God was there. He walked with them and you'll notice He never averted His eyes. That's because He made the nakedness beautiful.

After the Fall, that all came crashing down. God had to cover them as a reminder of their shame and fallen state—as well as, I suppose, the fact it was going to get chilly now. The environment wasn't perfectly regulated anymore. And everyone knows a cool breeze blowing on a naked person has never been conducive to looking glamorous.

Let's be honest, in cold weather, neither sex looks particularly attractive naked. Although, if the truth be told, cold weather does seem to do a lot more damage to the ego of the naked man.

When Adam and Eve first realized their predicament, they tried to cover themselves by using leaves. Leaves! Apparently, common sense was another attribute that took a dive after the Fall. I'm sure it also drove home a whole new awareness of their bodies' unique designs when they sat for the first time in their shrubbery underpants! God (who always seems to be one step ahead of us when it comes to this type of thing) immediately used fur to protect them from their new environment and to keep them warm.

That, by the way, is why we wore fur in the first place. Not to look chic, but for a more practical reason: WE WERE COLD! We needed fur! We don't possess it ourselves, but, thankfully, God had the insight to create little fur-making factories also known as animals. Fur became a necessity for survival. We couldn't have survived without it. I know there are some people in our society who don't like to hear that (I'll talk about them later), but it's a fact nonetheless.

You take the furriest guy you ever met (if you don't know one, go get your hands on a Middle Eastern fellow), set him next to a yak, and he'll look like the Dalai Lama!

We all know the ramifications of the Fall and all the hurt it caused and it wasn't just about fur. Something insidious took place there that is often overlooked. Not only did we as humans look at God differently by this loss of relationship, but we also looked at each other in a different light. Now, for the first time, Adam and Eve were very much aware of each other's looks! Not that they didn't enjoy the visual element of each other before; after all, God did look at Eve and say this was very good. But now they could also see the ugly side of being human. There was no longer pristine bliss, where they saw each other as intrinsically beautiful first. Nor was it the perfect world, where everyone was appreciated for exactly the way God created them.

No, from now on, humans were going to begin judging one another by outward appearance first! It began the practice of seeing humans as instrumentally valuable, as opposed to intrinsically valuable. Our bodies became property! And for the right price, they could now potentially be bought and sold. But to be valuable, it had to be desirable. This was laying the groundwork for all kinds of new evil. From the credit card (to buy body upgrades) to the impossible-to-answer-correctly phrase, "Honey, does this make me look fat?" the human race was doomed.

And no one has bought into the concept of our appearance being the primary gauge of assessing our value to society more than women. I feel sorry for them. There is a multibillion-dollar "beauty" product industry that thrives on a concept the very same industry continues to perpetuate. This is the myth that if you're female, your face, as is, is ugly! They have created a mood where many women refuse to be seen in public, sans makeup! Some women will actually tell you, "I can't go outside till I put my face on."

Look, ladies, I don't know if you're aware of this, but your face has been "on" from the get-go! Do you really believe no man has ever seen a woman without makeup?

How bad can it be that you are embarrassed to have someone see you in your natural state? Is your face really that horrific? If so, I would think male doctors would be freaking out at the very sight of this hideous monstrosity that just came out of the birth canal! They should be dropping baby girls left and right from fear! I can just imagine the chaos as they scream to the nurse, "Get some mascara on her immediately! She's repulsive! Quick! Put her face on so her parents can tell who she looks like!"

Now don't get me wrong, we men care about our looks too. We just haven't bought into the "makeup thing" to try and alter our appearances. Men seem to lean more into the elements of their body they believe represent their maleness. Hair, for instance, is a very important thing to men. Not hair in general, mind you, but the hair on our heads. Why that hair is the most important, I'm not sure.

Men can grow hair on their back, face, ears, and in their nose. Yet even if you are completely covered from head to toe, if it's not thick on your head, you're a loser.

That's the lie we bought. We bought it so hard we actually think we look better with a bad toupee than with a balding head. If there is a toupee on the market that looks good, I haven't seen it. Then again, if I saw it, it wouldn't be a good toupee, would it?

Toupees are designed, in theory, to draw attention away from the fact this guy doesn't have hair. Unfortunately, their phony appearance does the opposite of this intended purpose by forcing us to look at the guy's head, wondering the whole time if he actually thinks he's fooling us. He wants to cover what he actually looks like bald, and the toupee becomes a springboard for our imagination as we begin the arduous task of trying to imagine what the guy looks like without it.

I'll be honest. I happen to have a full head of hair, so I have never been put in the position of having to decide how I would respond if I were losing my hair. I would hope if I were losing it, I would simply allow myself the freedom to let the world see me as I am. But before you begin accusing me of self-righteousness for not having sympathy for something I haven't experienced, hold onto your hair!

I do resonate with the feeling of not being satisfied with my looks because, I'll admit, I'm short. Not *Wizard of Oz* short, but short nonetheless. I am five foot six, which means I am "below average" (whatever that means) in height. I, too, have been the victim of the dictates of society, which have decided I am not as desirable as the taller guy. It's even in our lexicon: women all dream of "tall, dark, and handsome," the opposite implication apparently being those who are "short, pale, and plain" might as well give it up. Now, that look might fly if I were Amish, but it definitely is not going to get me on the cover of *GQ*.

It also gives me a minority status only short people understand. Anyone who has been a minority in some way knows you do have to work harder to be seen as equally valuable. So I too am a victim of the Fall.

Now, I get to make a choice as to how I'm going to respond to this curse. I can play the victim or I can appreciate the challenge this sets before me. For example, I have always been forced to work harder than the next guy. Maybe that's a good thing. When you aren't given the obvious attributes of the beautiful people, you learn to adapt and fight. Of course, when you do try to stand up for yourself as a short guy, it's not seen as noble; it's referred to as a disease! It's called the Napoleon Complex! The theory is if you're short, you feel inferior and try to make up for it by being overly aggressive.

The problem with the theory is short people are treated with less respect and have to do something to be seen as equal! YOU GOT A PROBLEM WITH THAT?!!! How would you like it if society defined your behavior not as a stand for dignity but as a sickness! You ever heard of the Goliath Complex? Of course not! Everyone assumes tall people have it together! You could be the biggest dork in the world, but if you're tall, people assume you're probably some super athlete. You hear the same tired clichés: "You're so tall, do you play basketball?" What are they going to say to a short guy? "You're short, are you a jockey?" You see?

Ironically, I had two short guys of the clinical variety complain to me for using the word "midget" on one of my albums years ago. I never realized the word was degrading as I used it in the dictionary context. I asked this brother what he would prefer I call him, and he said they go by "little people." Now, growing up short, anyone calling me a little person is about to experience a headbutt to the groin (which is about where my head comes up to on a normal-heighted guy), which characterizes the issue of content over context I will elaborate on in another chapter. One man's honor is another man's insult.

But, fortunately, other than hair and height, the beauty industry hasn't found a lot of places to sell men on their inferiority. However, since we don't wear makeup in order to look better, they did decide we needed to smell better.

Cologne is one of the few men's products we have been led to believe is a need. I never understood this concept though. The advertisement would say things like, "Smells like a man." What does THAT mean?! I am a man! I already smell like me! I can smell like me for nothing! If you want to convince me to shell out fifty dollars for a scent, I want it to smell like something other than me! Otherwise, what's the point?

On the other hand, some of the scents that have become standards are ridiculous. Like, for example, musk. Why do I want to smell like the mating scent of something when, in its natural habitat, stinks? A man should smell like something we love! Remember the smell of the leather on a new baseball glove? That would work. The smell of grease would work, or, in a pinch, spray on some WD-40. Or how about a fresh pizza right out of the oven! That's the smell of baseball, football, and boxing. That's what I want to smell like. Or even a new car! Nothing beats the smell of a new car. How about a new car smell for humans? That smells like a man!

Anyway, if we understand humans in the U.S. put undue emphasis on their looks, then what is a follower supposed to appear like? This has become one of the most precarious traps U.S. Christians have fallen into. So much emphasis was put on what a genuine Christian was supposed to look like, it became more important than who we actually were! The places we were told to avoid became more important than the people who were already there and needed us. Everything about us had to be associated with our newfound faith.

If you drove a car, it had to have a fish on it. I remember driving through Illinois once and someone passed me at ninety miles an hour with a big fat vanity plate saying something like "IM4JESUS"! Now, I know they were going ninety because I was going eighty, and they blew me away! (Of course, I was in a rental, which had no fish on it, so I was exempt.)

What does any of that have to do with who we are as Christians? So much of what we as American Christians have come to associate with Truth is actually cultural tradition. Once again, we trade honesty for appearance. For example, Southern Baptists have long been known for their stand against drinking, smoking, and dancing. (Being a comedian, I can also vouch for the fact many of them are against laughing.) These three visible activities are considered not only inappropriate for anyone calling themselves a Christian but actual sins.

Now, no one could argue that at least two of these behaviors, drinking and smoking, can be very dangerous and unhealthy, whereas dancing, when attempted by some Baptists I've met, is only dangerous to those of us watching. Overall, people would be healthier if they didn't engage in those first two potentially addictive behaviors. But honest Christians, from whatever denomination (Baptists aren't alone in this), should ask themselves: Are these actually sins?

Equally important is, if someone chooses to engage in them, can they really be Christians? I chose these two habits to examine not because I want people necessarily to engage in them (that's not for me to judge) but because they are controversial and provide an example that can help us decide what template we should use when examining others' lifestyle indulgences.

Charles Spurgeon is a Baptist icon. His influence is so pervasive, and should be; I dare say some Baptist pastor somewhere in the country probably quotes him every week. He was a true committed believer, who God used mightily in England and whose reputation, as already noted, has been extremely pervasive here in the United States. No one would doubt for a minute he was a true follower of the living God. No one could deny his influence either. What also can't be denied is the fact Charles Spurgeon SMOKED CIGARS! Sometimes WHILE PREACHING!

Someone once asked him about it and he said he smoked in moderation. When they further pursued the issue by asking what he meant by "moderation," he responded, "I don't smoke two at a time." (Although I'd like to think Chuck was that clever, this line has also been attributed to Mark Twain.) What should we make of this fact? Was Spurgeon apostate or not? Of course, at that time no one knew the health dangers associated with smoking. Had Charles known that, would he have quit? Who knows?

Maintaining our health certainly is a noble and perhaps even godly pursuit. But before we get self-righteous in our condemnation, remember the Bible says nothing against smoking. So we have to use our reason and experience to try to decipher exactly where this gray area fits. It does bring up gluttony, though, and our country by far has more health issues with overeating than it does with smoking.

Again, one of the curses of living in the greatest nation on Earth is we have the option of getting fat! Most people in the world couldn't get fat if they wanted to! If we aren't a nation of abundance, who is?

I can't make this point more seriously. I know many pastors who don't drink or smoke and yet have serious weight problems. If you're going to use the "Your body is a temple" line to prove your case against bad habits or drinking, then you better take a good long look in the mirror. Some "temples" have some extra rooms added that weren't in the original architecture!

Now, don't get me wrong, I'm not trivializing this at all, nor am I judging. I'm making the point we have allowed in our cultural traditions not taking gluttony as seriously as the other sins of overindulgence. And that's exactly what we're dealing with here: lack of moderation. Look at dessert, for example. There is nothing healthy about a hot fudge sundae. Nothing! Its only purpose is for pure enjoyment. It's empty calories, high in fat, and overloaded with sugar. There is nothing about it one could claim as a benefit to one's temple. It's even joked about as being "sinfully good." We inherently realize we are eating these desserts simply because they bring us pleasure! We like the way they taste and we like the feeling we get when we indulge in them.

So we must ask ourselves, if we are consuming a food that gives our body no nutrition but is simply for our pleasure, then doesn't that sound very much like we are bordering on a sin? That is, if we believe doing something for the pleasure of it automatically constitutes sin. That is the crux of the matter. We have taken on a tradition that somehow our Heavenly Father doesn't want to see us enjoy ourselves. What a sad testimony to Christianity we've become if that is the legacy we've left to those who know nothing of God.

I have come to believe the exact opposite over the course of my life. God does give us things for our pleasure. A glass of wine, for example, is proven to be good for your heart. (Actually, science has said one drink a day of anything can be beneficial for us.) But the fact there is a relaxing element to it shouldn't make us see it as suspect. I mean, if you believe any medication given to you and prescribed by a doctor to help you relax or sleep or deal with anxiety is sinful, then why take aspirin when you get a headache? Maybe God wants your head to hurt? Yet we have taken a natural chemical from a tree that eventually becomes aspirin, and we see that as a God-given help to us. Guess what? Wine can do the same thing!

Ironically, Christians from Europe who might be reading this would be scratching their heads wondering what the fuss was about. In fact, I can think of one in particular who would.

Ever heard of C. S. Lewis? Who hasn't, since he's one of the greatest Christian apologists of the twentieth century? Who wouldn't consider it a great honor to spend time with this man discussing the Truths of Christ? Of course, that would also mean spending time in a local pub in front of a pint of beer because that was and is the customary meeting place for people from England.

Imagine seeing him there discussing God's thoughts across the table from one of his closest friends, J. R. R. Tolkien (who, by the way, helped lead Lewis to Christ), while they both indulged in some hearty English ale. To say that scenario didn't happen would be untrue; to say this behavior makes his literature suddenly illegitimate and suspect is so absurd it isn't worth the dialogue. The truth is, when the Bible speaks about alcohol, it never says don't drink; it says don't be a drunkard. There is an assumption of responsibility in moderation other religions don't even offer!

In many ways, this is similar to the prototype people.

Adam was given life to enjoy simply for the sake of enjoyment. God placed only one condition on it: "Don't eat from that tree." God says enjoy your sundae, Buffalo wings fried in grease, and, yes, your glass of beer. Just don't get drunk. It's up to you to moderate yourself. This is the price of living with the most liberal and freeing religion of all time: you can abuse it!

If staying away completely keeps you from doing just that, then you have made a choice based on your relationship with God. And good for you! All I am saying is it may not be mine. Even our culture puts certain restrictions on drinking, such as not being able to drink alcohol until you are twenty-one. So drinking before that age would be breaking the law, which means you have sinned.

Of course, there is always the idea of refraining from something because someone may stumble, but if having a drink fits into that category, then what do we do with Jesus, who not only drank wine but made it!? Did He sin? If not, then maybe this idea of a "stumbling block" means something different than how we have always understood it. Maybe we have defined it to mean something that has become another assumed truth—when it's actually something more mysterious than we can even begin to fully grasp.

By the way, just as an aside here—I am not making the argument an organization can't impose as one of its rules that one cannot imbibe while working under its particular ministry; I have no problem with that. If they have chosen a code of conduct that works for them and you don't like it, then don't work for them! I also realize some people reading this could use it as an excuse to start or continue overindulging. But that simply demonstrates they were somehow able to skip over the "don't get drunk" part the Bible does clearly command us to obey.

In fact, I am not trying to make a case for drinking alcohol at all; I am simply saying that turning something into a sin because YOU don't like it doesn't suddenly make it BIBLICALLY accurate. Of course, if you're still of the mindset that believes the oppressiveness of legalism is somehow honoring God, then your ability to not see yourself in the Pharisee is glaring. So, just for the record, I will say again that getting drunk is unhealthy, dangerous, possibly life-threatening to yourself and others, and not a good witness. In Jesus's day it was considered wrong behavior.

Now, I grant, getting drunk in Jesus's day certainly didn't have the repercussions we face today with cars and firearms available to all. To be driving drunk in an ox cart means the worst harm you probably could do is run over somebody's foot. The alcoholic beverage industry also has been very irresponsible in marketing liquor as associated with fun, youth, and social appeal. If you never pick up a drink in your life, you are probably better off in the long run.

But the dangers of drinking alcohol still do not make the act a sin! Jesus was accused of being a drunkard. This would be a hard accusation to make if Jesus never drank. For some of us in the U.S., this is still an extremely difficult fact to accept. This is why it's crucial we practice the art of discerning the difference between the Holy Spirit's conviction and our cultural traditions. The truth is sometimes what appears to be a sin or inappropriate Christian behavior simply ISN'T! It's culturally imposed, and sometimes that imposition is used by Satan to squelch an opportunity to WITNESS.

For example, I know a Christian who moved into a new neighborhood. He met a man who had moved there from another country, and this guy invited his new Christian neighbor out for a beer. The Christian said, "Sure, I would love to."

Immediately, the new neighbor said, "That's great. I gave the same invitation to another neighbor and they said they didn't drink because they were Christians." Remember, this person was from a country where everyone hangs out in pubs. During the visit the Christian had an opportunity to socialize with this new neighbor and his wife and, at one point, shared the Gospel with them for ten minutes.

Now, who was the better witness? The Christian who didn't connect with the neighbor and consequently had no relationship or the one who shared in the hospitality of some people who desperately needed Jesus? The sad part is we have a Christian who is able to smugly go to church and feel secure in the fact they "witnessed" to the pagan by ignoring their invitation of hospitality.

We are called to moderation and self-discipline, not to some false "proof" of your piety by some man-made ideas. Jesus made a ministry out of forcing the religious out of their self-imposed customs, by showing them restored relationships will always be demanded over self-righteousness. He wants us to connect others with God by proving our own relationship with God is defined by giving ourselves to others, not to some religious formula that distances us from the world.

In the Gospel of John we have an example of one such incident. Jesus was teaching in the temple one morning when the teachers of religious law and the Pharisees brought to Jesus a woman caught in adultery. The Bible actually says they caught her in the very act! Now, of all the sins a person could commit, and, believe me, they are numerous, if I had to single out one I would not want to be caught "in the very act" of, I pretty much think I would lean toward that one. Maybe it's me, but I'd much rather have my pastor see me robbing a convenience store than find me in bed with a woman who isn't my wife. To be honest, I'm not crazy about visualizing my pastor finding me in bed with my wife. "I love you, brother, now what are you doing in my bedroom?!"

Nevertheless, this was the position this woman found herself in the first time she met Jesus. At this point, shame was the least of her problems. There was a punishment everyone was aware of for the perpetrator of this crime and it wasn't to appear on an episode of *Judge Judy*. No, in that day and age, sin wasn't used as an intriguing episode of entertainment. Covenants were taken seriously between a husband and wife. Though apparently, as this scenario indicates, more was expected from the woman. Adultery wasn't used to blame someone else for not "meeting our needs"; instead, it was a one-way ticket to the stone pile.

Many sermons have been done on this story, usually relating to God's grace. But I'm more interested in the fact this woman was guilty. She broke a law Moses put into place. It was a real law and to break it was considered a sin. There isn't a Christian in the country today who wouldn't consider adultery a sin. Still, in all this legalism, Jesus found it more important to get this woman off the hook than to be true to the unyielding distribution of the law. In other words, He would rather forgive her. My point being not so much the awesome grace of God, which we've all exploited more than appreciated, but to look closely at the idea Jesus's response to this scenario was wrong! After all, if this woman actually sinned, why is it fair for her to get off? I'm sure there were plenty of people who didn't escape judgment over the years.

But, once again, the apparent truth is not everything that appears wrong to me necessarily is! Jesus constantly made it clear He was more interested in establishing a relationship of reconciliation with His creation than He was in punishment. Why else save all His harshest words for the religious? He hated the fact appearance took precedence over compassion. Laws are necessary as boundary markers for human behavior. But it seems God constantly trumps law with love.

Think about that. Even though the religious were doing what they were supposed to do, it was considered invalid because of their heart attitude! Perhaps I should be vulnerable enough to expose my own weakness in this area. I love a gin martini, ice-cold with three olives stuffed with bleu cheese! I love a single malt scotch, neat, with a cigar, even. I also love an ice-cold IPA microbrewed beer to round out a barbecue or attending a baseball game. I drank a few for years and I always did it with the boundaries of a good witness in mind. I never drank before work nor did I drink and drive or drink in the morning. But I did get used to a couple in the afternoon before dinner and it became a habit, a habit that lasted a long time.

My wife would try to gently encourage me to perhaps forgo a drink tonight. She had no problem with drinking and always said, "I just don't want it to become a problem for you. I want you to be able to have a glass of champagne at your daughter's wedding." In her desire to allow me my autonomy she found herself codependent and enabling my habit. It never felt wrong to me but over time I did find it changing my personality. I began to get darker and quick to anger.

Something about this habit was out of control and I either couldn't see it or didn't want to. My wife then began to complain about it and "nag" me about it until I found myself frustrated and angry that I as an adult man wasn't able to have a couple drinks in my own home. After all, I deserved it as I provided for my family and was just relaxing a bit.

One day I woke up to a pain on my right side. I immediately made the grave mistake of searching the symptom on WebMD. BTW, I found out the biggest cause of heart failure in the U.S. It's using WebMD to evaluate a physical symptom. The first story I came across was a man waking to a painful right side only to discover he had cirrhosis of the liver. Suddenly, all of my rationale, my excuses and my lying to myself, went out the window. I was convinced I had gone too far and I was dying of liver failure.

I don't know if any of you have ever suffered from a perception that you were dying, but I can only say it was as real to me as if my doctor said, "I'm sorry, Brad, get your affairs in order, you have six months." I began to get depressed and nothing could convince me otherwise. I had tests done at the actual doctor's office and everything came back negative, but I had a symptom, and no matter what the results were, I decided then it must be something else. I went from cirrhosis to colon cancer and beyond.

Long story short, I prayed to God and said this: "Lord, you don't owe me anything. If I am dying, I got there by my own choices. But, if by your grace you would see fit to heal me, I promise I will never drink again." Well, shortly thereafter it finally became clear I was fine. Now, did I have cirrhosis and was healed or was it all in my mind and I finally received scientific proof to validate it? I don't know. But as far as I am concerned, either way the result was the same. I was healed of cirrhosis.

I remember telling my mom this story and she said, "Yes, we all knew you were an alcoholic." WHAT?! I didn't know I was an alcoholic. In retrospect, though, it is clear to me I was. I tell you this story in order to help you see that even a true believer in Christ can fool himself into believing he is fine in order to indulge in his sin. I tell you this story to encourage someone who might be struggling with this issue themselves and to add that I have been completely sober since August 1, 2017!

I found out the hard way I am one of those people who simply cannot drink. Why? Because I am incapable of doing it moderately. If what God has shown me about this faith journey is to help others, then the truth is sacrosanct. Drinking is NOT a sin. But for some people, because they can't moderate themselves, it is. I'm sorry to say I'm one of them.

I wish I could still have my ice-cold IPA with chicken wings but those days are gone for me. You know what, though? I'm okay. I have the peace of knowing I do in fact desire God and His calling on my life more than my freedoms. All things are lawful to me but not all things are expedient. We as believers must get over the fleshly need to appear better on the outside than we actually are on the inside. There are situations where Christians judge other believers for what they perceive as backsliding when in fact the "backslider" is by far bringing more value to the kingdom. Do you think it should be obvious to tell the difference? I know a story that might give you pause. Read on.

SAINTS AND STRIP CLUBS

ASSUMED TRUTH 4: There are some places TOO sinful for Christians to enter.

What would you think if I told you I had a call to the mission field? Most followers would consider that a great sacrifice. We have all heard stories of people called to Africa or some foreboding place and we wonder if we would have the courage and faith to go to such a place at the behest of the Father. We envision an extremely backward culture compared to our standards—hot and desolate with people of completely different customs and experiences from us. We think about having to eat things they consider delicacies, which we would only eat on a bet!

Many of these natives would be naked, except for strange adornments puncturing their skin. If I told you this was the world I was going to place myself in, how many of you would say I shouldn't go? Not because they don't need Jesus but because they're naked and it could cause me to stumble.

Well, unless you're suffering from some brain disorder, it wouldn't even cross your mind! These are human creations Christ died for! The lack of clothing isn't even in the equation.

Now let me ask the same question with a slightly different spin. What if I told you I was called to a mission field of people who are from a completely different culture than me? Their worldview is completely unlike mine. They perform strange dances while naked, in order to incite our mortal passions. They take drugs and special liquid concoctions that induce strange thoughts and hallucinations and lower their moral inhibitions. It's a culture desperately needing Jesus. Should I go?

You would probably wonder why I would even ask. They sound like they need the Gospel desperately. The difference is this: I'm not talking about a South American jungle. I'm talking about a strip club in Hollywood, California! NOW is where our tradition immediately kicks in. Most Christians' first response, if they're honest, is, "No, that wouldn't be right." Then they will try to formulate compromises to achieve your call without sacrificing your integrity.

Perhaps, they might muse, you could offer a hangout afterward catering to these people, some special Wednesday night service sponsored by ex-strippers. Provide a shelter for them to come to you, but certainly don't go there!

Don't you find it interesting we have no problem considering someone's call to minister among naked natives "legitimate"? (After all, they are savages.) But we have big problems if the naked in question are fellow Americans!

By now you may be asking yourself two questions: (1) what's your point? and (2) why are you always bringing up naked people? Let me tell you a true story. This one takes place in the sixties, during the height of the "flower power" movement. Hippies roamed the streets, endorsing sex, drugs, and rock and roll. Nowhere was this more obvious than on Sunset Boulevard in Hollywood.

During this time there was a young Baptist preacher named Arthur, who established a small church for the hippies and homeless to come hear the Good News of Jesus. This guy walked up and down Sunset, witnessing to everyone he met and inviting them to his church. He always made it a point to introduce himself to any of the "players" in the area, nightclub owners, managers, and the like.

At that same time, there was a man named Ron Bozarth, who managed a nightclub on the strip. Not just any nightclub, mind you, but a topless nightclub. He, along with a partner, started, from what I understand, the first topless club in the country. They actually conceived and implemented the trend we are, sadly, so familiar with now in this country.

Arthur made it a point to introduce himself to Ron, all the while mentioning he heard Ron was "the man to know around here." Arthur also made a very strange statement to Ron only minutes after their first introduction. He said he believed God called Ron to preach. Now, I figure I'm fairly spiritual, but I must admit if I met the owner/manager of the first strip club in the U.S., I don't know that his call to be a pastor would have come to mind.

But that's just a little precursor to the boldness Arthur was imbued with. Arthur then made an even more unusual request. He asked Ron if he could go into the club and talk to his girls, to let them know if they ever needed a place to go or someone to talk to, he'd be there.

Ron, aided by his alcohol and speed addiction (which has long been heralded for its ability to help us make rational decisions), for some reason thought that would be a good idea. He also thought it would be funny to lock this preacher in the room with a half dozen naked women.

So he did.

After a while one of the waitresses went up to Ron to let him know there was a problem. None of the girls were dancing. Ron immediately raced back to the dressing room (kind of an inappropriate name for a room in a strip club, huh?) to find these women on their knees looking at the Scriptures Arthur was sharing. Ron blew up (to say the least), demanding the girls get their "butts and every other part of their visible torso" out onto the stage to dance.

Arthur then asked if it would be okay if he went and talked to his bartenders a little. "Sure," Ron said, just wanting to get him out of the way. Minutes later the waitress again came to Ron complaining that none of the drinks were getting out. Again, he saw Arthur over there with his Bible wide open, talking to his bartenders, who stood there enraptured by this wacky hippie man of God.

Again Ron blew up, demanding Arthur get lost so his people could make a living. Arthur then made one final request. Would it be all right if he went on stage between dances to tell the crowd about his church and that they were welcome to attend if they were so inclined? Believe it or not, Ron said yes!

This time, however, there was a method to Ron's madness. Ron knew full well he had a crowd waiting around the block to get into this most popular club. And he assumed if he let this fanatic on stage, it would drive some of the people out of the club, thus providing an opportunity to get a whole new batch of people in. All with cover charge in hand!

So Arthur took the stage—and twenty minutes later Ron had to yank him off again as he actually started a full evangelistic message! Right before Arthur jumped down, he told the audience this: "If anyone is interested in knowing Jesus Christ as Savior, you can meet with me at the back of the club."

Sounds rather far-fetched, doesn't it? Now, if you are a believer, I want you to honestly ask yourself what you make of that story. Are you wondering what good could possibly come out of this event? Think of all the people from Arthur's church who may have seen him come out of the club. Wouldn't they assume the worst? Was it worth taking a chance? Wasn't Arthur disregarding the biblical concept of avoiding all appearance of evil?

Yes, at first glance, it would appear the risk of damaging his reputation wasn't worth this excursion into the dark side. Remember, however, he was ministering to every bar and shop on the strip, and that included a strip club. There are some of you reading this who believe if Arthur were truly called by God to this place, he would have engaged in a much more common and "effective" way of ministering to the people.

First, he would have stood outside this den of iniquity, picketing and chanting slogans of God's disapproval. He also would have made it a point to hand out flyers and tracts telling customers about their impending destiny with hell. Now, I'm not saying every believer would feel led to enter a strip club and look for witnessing opportunities. What I am asking is, HOW DO WE KNOW SOME AREN'T?!

Maybe that's the reason God constantly tells us not to judge others—because we just don't have all the information! Do you disagree? Think I'm compromising my call to holiness? Well, let's go back to our story and see what results occurred.

Starting with that first sermon on the stripper stage, seven men got up and met Arthur at the back of the room, where they all gave their lives to Christ! Now, for those of us who question whether Arthur should have entered the club in the first place, why don't you wait and ask those seven brothers in heaven!? For those seven men, the answer is obvious, but that's just the beginning.

Many of the dancers of the club also became believers.

Any woman who degrades herself in front of men for money isn't necessarily a cut-and-dried hussy; she's more than likely hurting, usually as a result of an abusive or nonexistent relationship with her earthly dad. After realizing how much they were treasured by their Father in heaven, many began new lives, even starting families of their own.

Those were some of the results of that one night!

Whatever happened to Arthur, you might ask? He attended a seminary, where he was kicked out because of his unorthodox witnessing choices. See, Arthur made it a practice to enter any and all establishments that met only one particular criterion—they were inhabited by humans. Of course, that included lots of places where the humans were drinking and smoking.

Imagine someone claiming to be a true follower of Jesus yet going into nightclubs to witness! What would any self-respecting church board think of a Christian actually having the audacity to choose a place filled with sinners to witness? What is he?

Nuts? Doesn't he realize Jesus called us to wait for sinners to show up in church so we can let the pastor witness to them in the form of an altar call? All that was expected of us was to have every head bowed and every eye closed, you know, so no one feels embarrassed. (That is, until the sinners are asked to raise their hands—then we have to peek.)

But the Lord had a plan for Arthur and, interestingly enough, He didn't see the need to ask the rest of us for approval. Anytime God finds someone willing to go and do what He calls him to, no matter what flack he receives from fellow Christians, God knows He's found a living sacrifice. And usually God's got special plans for these lunatics. Arthur was no different. One night while Arthur was praying, God told him (I know, I've never heard God's voice either; then again, I've never witnessed in a strip club) to pull the large cross off his wall and carry it as he walked on foot across the country.

And, of course, Arthur being Arthur, said yes. On Christmas Day, 1969, Arthur picked up his cross, literally, attached a wheel to it, and began to walk east. Now, these many years later, if you look at a copy of *Guinness World Records 2015*, there you will find a picture of Arthur Blessitt, a man who has the longest documented walk by a human being of all time! He has literally been in every nation on Earth with his cross, preaching the Gospel.

Finally, what about Ron, the club owner who began the strip club trend in America?

I saw him every Sunday for five years at Christ Fellowship, the church I attended in Lake Forest, California. He wasn't a parishioner—he was my pastor. I'm sorry to say Pastor Ron has passed away since those wonderful days I attended his church, but his teachings and his giving heart will always remain with me. That's the church where my wife was saved.

When I first heard this story in the form of a testimony, I realized my own story is similar, though not nearly as courageous. Any believer who finds himself drawn to the arts usually discovers he's in a never-ending dilemma of battling with secular mentality that doesn't necessarily want what he's selling and a religious mentality that doesn't want him selling it there. As a professional comedian for thirty years, I found I had to work twice as hard to establish my career calling.

Not only was I like everyone else who was trying to learn my craft on stage in front of a sometimes hostile, usually drunk crowd, but, as a believer, I did my show 100 percent curse-free!

When you are in a club setting and the comedians in front of you have all used the "F" word about three hundred times apiece, it's extremely difficult to get on stage without cursing and without gratuitous sexual references and have the crowd stay with you. Once the style of comedy has been established as extremely graphic, which caters to the basest side of our fallen nature, it's difficult to pull people back into the light.

But this was my mission. Instead of fleeing the scene and trying to find a crowd that wanted clean comedy, I knew I was going to have to learn to compete on the secular level. I wanted people to see how good clean comedy could be and if no one else was going to provide it, I'd give it a shot.

After all, if you want to be great at comedy, you have to go where the best comedy is displayed. And I've got a flash for you, that isn't in a church! One of the great things about comedy is it allows you the latitude to say anything you want, as long as it's funny or in context with your style. I found myself constantly using biblical metaphors and topics on stage, everything from the story of Adam and Eve to the "God is my co-pilot" bumper stickers.

Being clean on stage wasn't really the witness I hoped it would be, because most people weren't even aware I was witnessing! They just came to laugh and didn't really care what package the laughs came in.

In the last years of the bulk of my work coming from comedy clubs, I closed my show by saying, "Well, I've been up here forty-five minutes and didn't use one curse word. They said it couldn't be done, but I do it every night because I believe creativity is funnier than crude." Do you know what the crowd did?

They applauded! You see, sometimes the secular mind is looking for someone to set boundaries and standards they can respect. But we have to be able to do that with a standard of excellence they will appreciate. If I hadn't been funny, nobody would have listened to me, let alone allowed me to get on their stage. You have to earn the right to be heard.

Oftentimes fellow comedians were more aware of what I was doing than the audience. Anyone who has done comedy professionally knows it's tremendously more difficult to do it clean than dirty, and there were many times when fellow comedians talked to me after the show stating they too were thinking of "cleaning up their show." It was almost as if they were convicted, although I know the truth is they respected my clean approach only because they understood how hard it is to write that way.

I remember a comedian who was very dirty spending the week we worked together asking me why I was clean. I told him, "I am a Christian, but I also think it makes for more creative art." He couldn't believe I could be a Christian and be in clubs. He thought the two were mutually exclusive. (Sound familiar?) I continued to witness to him about my beliefs but I also witnessed through my craft. Sometimes you get further honoring God by your commitment to Him than you do talking about Him.

When the week ended, we went our separate ways. Ten years later, a comedian came into a club I was working to audition. He asked me if I remembered that particular guy, the one I'd worked with years ago. I said I did, but I hadn't seen him in years.

"Well," he said, "he told me to tell you he was sorry for being so hard on you the first time you met. He also wanted me to tell you he is married now, he's a Christian, and he only performs completely clean."

So there you have it. Did this guy become saved strictly because of me? Of course not! But for one moment in time, I was where I was supposed to be. A field ripe for harvest that had no farmers because for years Christians would rather let this particular crop rot than bring it into the barn! I was a piece of the machine God constructed to bring another of his children home. It only occurred because I was on the mission field of a nightclub.

The time has come for believers to understand we all have a part in the Body and some of those parts are going to end up in places we for years haven't been allowed to venture into. Instead of honoring those parts, many have tried to lop them off! As a matter of fact, some parts we are even embarrassed to talk about! We have no problem exalting the eye or for that matter the heart. Heck, even the spleen isn't so bad, but please don't talk about the colon!

That's how some believers seem to see ministries and calls of God they don't understand. They're colons! You know, folks, we all have colons and I don't know about you, but I'm rather fond of mine. To tell the truth, I desperately need it! Yet, instead of acknowledging their usefulness, believers have tried to ignore them or, worse yet, they try to stop them from functioning. How? By refusing to pray for them and by tearing them down. By trying to instill their take on what these parts should be doing. By deciding for them and everyone else what is the appropriate package for a Christian.

All the while these believers—these varying parts of God's Body—are accomplishing great things for the kingdom. The Word says there are many members but one Body, and no one—NO ONE—can tell any other part of the Body they are not needed. Some Christians, because of their archaic beliefs, become unwitting agents to constipate the well-oiled machine God desires to see in action!

I've spent my life as a performer in places many Christians fear to go. They considered me as inhabiting a place I was not supposed to be. I know there are many other fellow "colon Christians" out there doing the same thing. And despite what any person tells them, they are exactly where they are supposed to be.

I long for the day when believers don't judge others who are called into the secular world. Instead, they embrace it. I long for the day when we reach a place where we expect to find believers in the most unexpected places—where we support, by prayer and participation, fellow believers who are simply doing the best they can to be valuable to society—and the Church. I pray for the day when we as a Body finally renew our minds when it comes to what we expect from the rest of our appendages.

For Christians whom God happened to choose for the "limelight," I look forward to the day they can pursue their

God-purposed vision without having to be subjugated to that pathological religious response so many have had to endure, which I refer to as the "Amy Grant syndrome." Never heard of it? Buckle up; my next chapter isn't for the faint of heart.

FAME, FAILURE, AND PHARISEES

ASSUMED TRUTH 5: Christians in the entertainment industry cannot act, sing, or perform in anything that doesn't have a "Christian" message.

I have a real hard time with "celebrities." I have an even harder time with the concept of celebrity. No one in our society is more overrated. Yet, if you were going to try to gauge who is given the most amount of praise and recognition in our country, it would without a doubt go to people in the entertainment industry: actors, musicians, and, if you consider sports as entertainment, athletes. By the same token, if you were going to gauge who gets paid the most disproportionate amount of money for contributing the least to society, it would also go hands down to people in the entertainment industry. I'm not saying these folks aren't talented, mind you, or that entertainment isn't useful in society. But what I am saying is if from this day forward there was never another actor born on this earth, life would continue, people would still be happy, and no one would even care eventually.

Unfortunately, however, it's the people in this glamorous profession (along with the media, where they are catered to and given adulation and praise, as well as lots of fame, power, and prestige) who have some of the most influence on society in general. To adolescents, who are just trying to get through life without completely hating themselves, the entertainment industry is a dream world many would give anything to enter. What I keep asking myself is, why?

What exactly makes these people so appealing to others? Is it their intelligence? I mean, don't they always have a noble cause they stand for? Look at models; they're in a profession that worships clothing! Can there be an industry with less meaning? Clothing is simply designed to protect us from the elements and make it possible to have a place to wear a tie that looks reasonable.

A tie, by the way, is about as worthless as it gets. Doesn't keep you warm, falls in your soup, all the while doing its best to keep you from breathing! Boy, that's something we couldn't live without. Why not just wear a noose? We already discovered the first functional clothing was fur; yet what are models always spouting at us? "Don't wear fur!" You know why they can say that? Because look where models live! Los Angeles, Monte Carlo! Of course they say don't wear fur—they don't need it!

I know, let's have the next big model convention in Montana in the middle of January! Suddenly, you'll have all these lovers of nature screaming, "KILL SOMETHING!!! I don't care if it's endangered! Cut it open, I'm jumping in!" These are the same people, mind you, who will wear leather. Leather is dried meat! They will spend five hundred dollars to wear beef jerky with a zipper! That's just wrong!

Models also want you to know how difficult their job is. "Oh, it's so much pressure!" they'll say. I don't get it. How complex are their instructions? "All right, girls, walk to the end of the ramp, don't walk off, turn around, and come back." For that they get paid a hundred thousand dollars? You want proof your culture is crumbling from within? A model makes more in an hour of walking than a teacher makes in five years!

I won't even comment on the obscene amount of money an actor makes. Actors, however, may not be completely responsible for their actions. They all seem to suffer from the same disease that apparently is native to their Hollywood environment. If you're not familiar with it, it's called "De Niro-itis." It affects only the brain and manifests itself in the delusion that your profession as an actor somehow makes you smarter than those of us who aren't.

It's perpetuated in the fact that almost everyone in that community has the same progressive biases when it comes to social order, ethics, and morals. Anyone who dares venture out of their orthodoxy and have a dissenting view is instantly ridiculed, lambasted, and denied work, all in the name of "tolerance."

For some, like when I watched comedian Dennis Miller years back, they seem to contract it but their body begins to defend itself with natural antibodies, which in Latin are referred to as *conservativis mor communus sensis*. He, with a few other actors, appear to have changed their political views, which ironically coincided with our country being attacked by lunatics.

Sometimes shock treatment is the only cure for progressives who still believe the best way to confront terrorists is to reason with them. Yes, nothing more reasonable than a religious zealot with fifty pounds of plastic explosive strapped to his butt. Although Miller still seems to have some residual

De Niro-itis showing up in the form of his social worldview, I have faith someday he will be completely cured.

Unfortunately, for the likes of Michael Moore, Rob Reiner, and Bette Midler, the disease has advanced to the stage where their brains have completely been destroyed and the disease appears to be terminal. Their only chance for recovery would be to move to a new environment where they can live amongst like-minded people, where they won't feel so abnormal. North Korea comes to mind, but anywhere in the Middle East would probably be a better fit. If they're short on cash, I'm sure France would love to embrace them. Remember, the French were the ones who thought eating snails would be a good idea.

The reason this disease is never cured is the public at large feeds the problem by displaying its codependency when it comes to these people's images. Think of the terms we use to define them: "idols" (something we worship); "stars" (this huge mass of glorious light); "superstars" (just in case a "normal" star wasn't bright enough); and "icon" (given religious prestige). It's a profession that caters to, exalts, and rewards ego.

Coincidently enough, God told us the sin He hates most is…pride. And pride is nourished by ego. But surely someone so praised and well paid is good at what they do? So what is it exactly actors are good at? They entertain, sure, and that's good, but they don't even write their own words! They make a living using other people's words. Even more disturbing, their skills are in acting! This basically means they excel at pretending to be someone else! In their world it's called acting; in our world it's called schizophrenia! They seem to have no ability to think for themselves; this manifests in the fact the majority of them have or support a progressive agenda.

These are people who desperately want to be known as "artists." They want to consider themselves bohemians and are constantly parroting the fact they're counterculture and "different." Hate to burst your bubble, folks, but you're not "different" at all. In fact, you're exactly like everybody else who thinks like you, which is about 99 percent of Hollywood. You're essentially a cult of non-thinkers who are passionate about your point of view—as soon as Oprah Winfrey or Alyssa Milano tells you what it is.

That in itself isn't the problem. This wonderful country offers the luxury to believe whatsoever you will. But celebrity views don't represent America. The last election demonstrated that the majority of Americans are still more Conservative in their views. Why isn't this represented in Hollywood? The obvious answer is the powers that be in the fictitious "land" of Hollywood actually have an agenda: to destroy anything that passed for morality during the first 150 years of this country's formation. This is easy to accomplish when you already have people unable to formulate ideas outside the rhetoric of the propaganda Hollywood thrives on.

The hypocritical element of their worldview "arguments" is what is most glaring. They apparently hate big business and capitalism, although they are filthy rich themselves, and are governed by studios that are huge corporations. They feel Conservatives (by the way, all progressive ideology is formulated by feelings, not rationality) don't care about the homeless and they demand we be taxed to compensate for this oversight. In the meantime, they live in Malibu, in a secluded and gated community where they can live in hedonistic pleasure. Of course, they will claim they need protection from people who might try to break into their homes—you know, those people who don't have homes of their own. The very people they are so sympathetic to are the same ones they are protecting themselves from.

Does the term "disingenuous" ring a bell? Why don't they take 90 percent of their income after taxes and give it away to charities, all the while living in a modest home in Oxnard? No. That would mean they would have to suffer for their alleged cause as opposed to just using it to gain the "virtue cred" and photo ops, which garner them publicity between lunches at the latest hot spots. How can an industry be so narcissistic it has thirty or more awards shows a year to honor these "stars" as they walk the red carpet wearing dresses costing over a quarter million dollars and then have the audacity to act like they care for the underprivileged?

They constantly talk of the First Amendment (I can guarantee you most never read it) as though it's sacred to them. I for one am sickened by those who exploit the First Amendment but are not willing to fight for it; they are Americans but definitely not the type of Americans who created this country. The biggest reason they have such an influence on society is not that they are necessarily better or more talented than the rest of us. It's the fact their profession allows them to play characters who aren't real. They always get the funny line when they need it. They play heroes and courageous characters.

Their roles as actors create the illusion they are funnier than us, more romantic than us, more interesting than us. Your average American laborer accepts this illusion as representative of who these people actually are and is willing to spend his hard-earned money to subsidize their lifestyle, a lifestyle most of us will never know.

We Americans seem to value personality over character, and it is becoming our undoing. There is an old saying in Hollywood: "I don't care what they say about me as long as they spell my name right." There is seemingly nothing an actor can do that will keep him from getting hired in Hollywood! Do drugs, be an alcoholic, cheat on your wife—nothing is off limits! Yet when they go back to the set of their sitcom playing the role of a funny, loving father, that is the image America accepts. Is it because America is such a forgiving nation, or just a shallow one?

The power of celebrity is unfathomable. I remember being in line at Disneyland once to go on the Peter Pan ride when Hugh Hefner got off the ride with three blondes under his arms. People went nuts, taking pictures, staring in awe and amazement! I wanted to point out: he PUBLISHES A PORNO MAGAZINE!! He is the one telling your daughter her value is in her sexuality! If you are a celebrity in the U.S., short of murder, there is nothing you can do to garner our disfavor.

What is most disturbing is these people wouldn't have a voice if the Conservatives and Christians in this country stopped watching their TV shows, going to their movies, and buying the products of the sponsors who fund them. How about a silent protest? Not a protest by waving placards, mind you, but by hitting 'em where every committed progressive suddenly gets amnesia when it comes to standing for his cause, the pocketbook.

I remember seeing a television talk show years ago where Tim Robbins was talking about the pain he's endured trying to be able to work after the backlash he and his cohabitational unit took for their stance against the war in Iraq and their anti-Bush diatribes. "I believe in a country where we should be able to believe whatever we want and not have work taken away from us," he said, or something to that effect. It was hard for me to catch everything between my momentary bouts of laughter and throwing up. Here is a guy who works in Hollywood, where for years those who are Conservative have been denied work or, at the least, told to shut up about their belief system.

Yes, the life of a progressive celebrity (redundant) must be tough when suddenly what you believe comes with a cost. I just hope he can somehow get over this trauma while he's in Cannes this year, eating caviar and drinking champagne. I'll be praying for ya, Tim! I can't imagine a world where your behavioral choices are never held up to scrutiny.

But there is a celebrity world where those rules do not exist, a place where the celebrity is beholden to his fans. Where the followers of a performer are constantly scrutinizing every move, and where they decide what is and isn't an appropriate career move.

I'm talking about the celebrity who also happens to be a Christian. If there is any profession that challenges your ability to hold your ego in check, it's the entertainment industry. Yet what about the Christians in this country who have been called to this very world? They have also been given the gift and, henceforth, the passion and desire to utilize their talents on stage.

When I started to perform stand-up comedy full-time in 1988, I didn't plan on performing in churches. As a matter of fact, it never even entered my mind. I have always been of the mindset that with whatever dream one follows the only expectation should be to strive for excellence.

Especially as representatives of the creator of art, we should accept nothing less than greatness. Jesus spoke the parable of the talents where the most honor was bestowed on the one who did the most, and likewise influenced the most, with his talent. There was an expectation by the giver of the talent that it be used for greatness. The talent was always owned by the ruler but was entrusted to the servants. Not so they could spend it on themselves but so they could make the most out of it as representatives of the giver.

Christians over the years have had the tendency to create a box all of Christendom is expected to work out of. I told you already of the time I was insulted by a fellow church member, simply because I enjoyed performing for people and chose the art of sleight of hand to usher me into that world of entertainment. As I have said, I now know her comment was made out of ignorance, but I was eighteen, still suffering from those teenage low self-esteem issues as well as the pain of my parents' divorce, and there was very little safe ground I could escape to. This was just another moment when I felt that who I was, who I longed to be, was open to manipulation by someone I trusted.

Funny how one innocuous statement by someone, who I'm sure never thought of it again, can stick with you all your life. What it also did for me, I might add, was force me to search out my faith for answers, to find out if what I was doing, and wanted to do as a profession, was appropriate. It forced me to come to grips with the fact a true follower does have an obligation to seek Truth, no matter how it might disagree with our desires.

A few years after being deflated by the church lady, as I was perusing a Christian magazine, I came across an article on Amy Grant. I don't remember all of it, but what I do remember was Amy had to defend herself because she wore a leopard print jacket on an album cover. She spoke of the fact she found the fabric, liked it, and made the jacket herself! If making your own clothes doesn't fit into the "domestic, maternal, family values mold," what does she have to do? Shear the sheep and weave the fabric from a loom? Christians were lambasting her because they thought the jacket was, I don't know, "racy." Probably taken from a little-known verse in Hezekiah that strictly forbids women to wear clothes that have the appearance they were made in the century they inhabit.

My first thought was, "It's just a jacket!" But at that moment I felt a real affinity for her. Remember, in the early eighties, she was becoming the first of the so-called Christian stars. Here was a woman, obviously a believer, who had to defend herself and prove her legitimacy as a follower, simply because of the whims of Christians who feel their purpose in life is to seek out inappropriate Christian behavior and hold your feet to the fire until you repent and correct yourself. We aren't talking theology here; we are talking a JACKET! Kind of what I suspect Jesus had in mind when He talked about "straining at a gnat."

The older I get in my walk, the more I am convinced that many of the people with that type of Spirit will never see the gates of heaven. They will be the ones who will have to stand in front of the living God, crying out, "Did we not cast out demons in Your name? Did we not follow in Your name?"

And the answer will be, "Yes, you did it in My name. The problem is, I never knew you!" Anyone can use someone's name for anything; that doesn't mean they are legitimate heirs to that family. Sometimes claiming kinship to someone is called FRAUD! Stealing an identity that is, in fact, NOT yours yet using it to obtain wealth and prestige by being associated with an honorable family name not actually your own is fraudulent.

After reading the Amy Grant interview, I remember feeling very emotionally protective of her for some odd reason. Something inside me vowed that if we ever met someday, I wanted to say to her, "I'm sorry." Sorry for all the pain I am sure she has endured from fellow family members. I felt a bond, an empathy for her that seemed to echo things, surely on a smaller scale, that I, too, had felt. As I began to analyze this feeling, I kept it to myself, realizing that no matter how I felt this was God-given empathy, it would appear to everyone else as the first stages of a stalker!

Little did I know that one day I would actually get the chance to give her this moment. It was at GMA (Gospel Music Association) Week, and I was asked by Word Records to emcee a showcase event of their talent. I remember many of the great acts were on the bill—Salvador, 4Him, Nicole C. Mullen, among others. But I was amazed to see the headliner that evening was none other than Amy Grant.

I remember being in a hotel room, rehearsing what material I would do between acts, as well as how each one should be introduced. When I came to Amy, an idea began to take shape. I wasn't going to just give her credits; I was going to say something from the heart. Something I had waited to say to her personally for years I was going to have a chance to

75

say to her in front of thousands. I can't tell you exactly what I said that night but it went something like this:

> Our last act of the evening was probably the first real superstar in the Christian music field. The fact that all of you are sitting out there on big fat wallets is a direct result of the impact she has had on this industry. Yet I remember when she decided to wear a particular outfit she thought was appealing and was accused of being a sellout. When she began to make some secular songs singing with world-class secular artists, so she could reach a larger audience and provide herself an opportunity to be salt and light in the world, which is our purpose as believers, she was accused of backsliding!
>
> All the while she never said a word, never defended herself. But she is a singer. I happen to be a comedian. If someone did that to me, I would ask him to spend five minutes contemplating exactly what good he thinks he has done for the kingdom of God. And while he's at it, he should take another hour and a half and start pulling the logs out of his own eyes, the self-righteous jerk!! (Subtlety is not my strong suit!) I am proud to call her a Christian and prouder to call her my sister. Ladies and gentlemen, please welcome Amy Grant!

At this point I was a little nervous, not knowing if what I just did was going too far or not. But what happened next, I'll never forget. The crowd rushed the stage, taking pictures, applauding, and giving her a standing ovation! I remember thinking, as I observed from off stage, after eighteen years I finally was able to complete my vow to this talented believer and lift her up as I believed she deserved. What was even more interesting to me is how God never allows even a most sincere moment as that was for me to be clouded in ego.

I would have loved to say that after the show I was able to meet Amy and tell her why I did that. That suddenly she and I became close friends and started having breakfast together at Pancake Pantry, and when we weren't golfing, we would hang out at all the trendy Christian parties where everyone was indulging in sweet tea and Diet Coke.

But in the end, I never actually met Amy. Shows like that become very crowded and confusing. I did meet her husband though; apparently, he is in the music business too. I believe he called himself "Vince" Somebody or Other. He shook my hand and said thanks; I always appreciate a husband looking out for his wife.

I then walked out of the back of the Ryman Auditorium and went home. My mission was done. I was given a moment to let the Christian world know that, yes, Christians in the spotlight do have an extra responsibility for their behavior. We are representing Jesus in a high-profile way and understand we will be scrutinized. But when it's all said and done and the dust has settled, please remember something.

We, too, are humans, working out our salvation with fear and trembling. We are not and never will be perfect! If we minister to fellow followers, that is our calling, but we need those same followers to pray for US, minister to US, and give grace to US! None of us feel worthy of the place we have been put by God, and we certainly don't often feel especially qualified. All we said was, "We will go." Without the ministering of the Body, however, we are sure to fail.

Please remember you are on our side and we hurt just as you do. We are on a journey, and we are not asking to lead it. We simply ask you to take our hand as we travel. You know, just as you need.

CAN I SAY "SEX" IN CHURCH?

ASSUMED TRUTH 6: All "true" Christians
will be offended by the same things.

I have nipples! One on each side of my chest, and, unless you make your living in a sideshow, my prediction is: so do you! Women also have nipples. Even, from what I understand, Christian women!

Now, let's try an experiment. I want you to ask yourself a question: What was your first response to my opening paragraph? Be truthful and honest with yourself. What was the first thing you felt? Did you laugh? Were you confused, wondering what I was getting at? Or did you just wake up from a short nap that reading my book caused you to fall into and now you're dazed and bewildered, glancing at the guy in the seat next to you, hoping you weren't snoring?

Any one of those responses would be normal and, quite frankly, expected. (Especially the one where you keep nodding off.)

But there is one response I am particularly interested in, one I am sure many of you felt. You felt embarrassed, uncomfortable, and perhaps a little put out because you found a word inappropriate to mention. For those of you who find yourselves in that category, this chapter isn't for you; it's about you. Why? Because I think that type of attitude has been extremely prevalent in the Church for a long time, and this selfsame learned attitude has done a grave disservice to the effectiveness of the Body of Christ in reaching the nonbeliever! It's not only non-biblical, it's just plain immature! There. I said it and I'm glad!

Experiment number two: How did you respond to the last statement accusing you of immaturity? I do have some good news for those of you who are angry but intrigued enough to keep reading: you are already moving out of that world! You see, one of the greatest characteristics we can cultivate as humans is to get to a place where what we believe is NEVER more important than what is true! Now, I hope I have brought you to a place where you are willing, even anxious, to hear my argument. But what is the argument about and how does it apply to nipples? (There's that word again.) Actually, nipples have little to do with it; they aren't important. Are you ready for the revelation?

For too long, the progressive ideologues in this country have created an environment that has taught us to judge content over context! Even followers (who should be the most liberal thinkers in society) have fallen into this trap! As a professional comedian, I have learned this truth firsthand. An audience can hear a word they don't like and immediately cease to listen! This is the great truth that needs to be explored. What is said is never important; what is important is what is meant! Why? Because words are purveyors of ideas. They aren't in and of themselves where the power lies; they are the vehicles carrying the power to the listener.

One of the great revelatory freedoms God gave me in my life was the verse 1 Corinthians 6:12. Listen carefully to this as it could change your life. "All things are lawful to me, but all things are not expedient: all things are lawful to me, but I won't be brought under the power of any."

This is HUGE! It is a formula to help you gauge whatever path you're about to tread. All things are lawful, but since, as we have observed, many gray areas cause us to wonder if God would approve, we simply need to explore our actions in this way: IS WHAT I'M ABOUT TO DO OR SAY EXPEDIENT TO MY LIFE PURPOSE, WHICH IS TO REPRESENT CHRIST IN THE MOST EFFECTIVE WAY POSSIBLE?!

What if you wanted to go into a nightclub and wondered if God would want you there? Ask yourself what your motivation is for entering. Am I going in to get drunk and hit on some single member of the opposite sex? Then I would guess you could pretty much rule that out as an expedient motivation. But what if the reason you're going in is to meet a neighbor you know hangs out there because you want him to see you and be blown away by your presence, since he always believed Christians weren't allowed in such dens of iniquity? Watch his countenance change as you tell him you want to be his friend, and the great thing about true Christianity is it allows you to do many things people used to think were wrong in order to show him a relationship is really what God wants with him. What if what you really want to do there is let him know God reveals His desire for relationship to humans through humans?!

Now, it's very possible someone from your church will see you coming out of this place and wonder what you're doing there. His maturity will reveal itself based on his first response. If he has a mature faith, he will respond in one of a few possible ways:

- He will assess your life fruit and assume you were there for a legitimate reason.
- He will approach you with it, saying he wondered if your presence was appropriate there because you're representing Jesus. (This is the least chosen response because it means the person has to be adult enough to come to you face to face.)
- He will just judge you and begin to gossip.
- He's coming out of the same place and is trying to keep you from seeing him!

In my experience dealing with Christians, if there is one element that seems most to be missing in our social intercourse amongst brethren, it's the fact that rarely do we approach each other face to face to dialogue over issues on which we disagree.

I once stood by my booth signing autographs for hundreds of guys at a Promise Keepers show. This guy walked up to me and handed me a note saying I should read it later. I have learned whenever a "Christian" does that, what they wrote is going to be condemnation. Sure enough, this saint had the insight to tell me the burning of *Harry Potter* books was a positive message, just as when they did it in Acts. This is another example of "Assumed Truth," which has led so many down the garden path of assumption. Then they get to the end of that path and have the hose turned on them.

First of all, anyone who believes in Jesus and can actually reason that book burning is a positive display of faith is in serious need of intervention! But it illustrates "Assumed

Truth" perfectly. Someone read the story of books being burned and simply took at face value that method must be the appropriate way for believers to deal with literature they think is antithetical to God's Commandments. But that is the problem.

So many Christians take just such a shallow approach to apologetics. We are supposed to "study to show ourselves approved unto God, a workman that needeth not be ashamed, rightly dividing the Word of Truth" (2 Tim. 2:15). Why did this pseudo-theologian read a story yet obviously take no time to analyze its meaning? This is why context is the crux of every dialogue, which can actually leave the participants with a greater understanding of Truth than what they started with.

The context of Acts was that those who consciously practiced witchcraft made the decision to renounce this ideology. To prove their new allegiance to Jesus, they made a public display of burning (now this is important) their own books! No Christian was grabbing their books from them and burning them. They chose to do it to make a public declaration of an internal spiritual transformation. Their act was similar to what we do when we are baptized. Baptism doesn't save us; it represents the way our soul has been changed inwardly.

Let me give you a story as an example. I once wore a shirt with a patch on it located over my nipple. As the day progressed, this patch began to rub against it and consequently chafe it. In other words, it hurt! Walking into church, I commented to a friend my nipple hurt, and he, in a panic, said, "Shhhh! Keep it down. We're in church!"

Okay, my prayer is most of you out there find his comment humorous, not because I said "nipple" (for the umpteenth time, definitely setting the world's record for the word "nipple"

83

being used in a book read primarily by Christians) but because he thought the word was inappropriate to say in church! He instantly responded to what I'd said without giving thought to the truth of the statement.

And what was the truth, you may ask? My nipple hurt! That truth didn't offend him; speaking the truth did! He was more concerned about what people might think if they heard the word than what was actually bothering me! Perception took precedence over my pain! That can't be right, especially when we analyze the scenario. This is a clear-cut case of legalism in a nutshell. Why? Because I don't want to attend any church more concerned about the fact I said "nipple" than the fact my nipple hurt! You don't have to pray for it; you don't have to lay hands on it. That would be awkward.

In our society, women cover their breasts in public, since having them exposed would be considered immodest. In New Guinea and parts of Africa and South America, this is not the case. Women don't cover their breasts and the people still somehow manage to get saved. These people have pragmatically created a logical dress code conducive to their environment. The context is the men of the tribe see breasts as more maternal than sexual. This makes sense when viewed outside our customs, although I admit if my mom moved to Death Valley and suddenly started walking around without a top, it would take some getting used to.

Nevertheless, we have created a cultural norm that works for us. Any context in which a woman removes her shirt in public in America would be considered a sin to the Christian mind, as there is no context in which this would be appropriate. Or is there? What about the case of women who are breast-feeding their children? The possibility of public exposure is not as important as having discovered the "revelation" their breasts have a God-given, beautiful function—the giving of life-sustaining sustenance to a newborn human.

The content (the abrupt appearance of a woman's breast) suddenly is not nearly as important as context—the desire to utilize this body part for the purpose for which it was intended. This makes it appropriate, if sometimes awkward, for the men who happen to be in the vicinity. Not knowing where to look, we find in ourselves the desire to respect this personal moment, and avoiding her gaze makes the fact we feel awkward even more obvious.

We don't want to embarrass the woman—but why should the woman be the one who feels embarrassed? If anyone should be embarrassed about having nipples it should be guys because we don't know what ours…do! They're duds! Yet we are the ones walking around with no shirt every summer without concern. "Look at these items I have for no reason whatsoever." I'm a freak and I don't care!

I often wonder what makes Christians choose the areas of society they find offensive. The kind of words we use have always been important to the image of Christians. We have never considered curse words to be appropriate and rightly so! The fact is there are some inappropriate words because by context they were designed to malign or inflame the person or group they are hurled at.

This is exactly the reason I never cursed in my show. It wasn't part of my language system. But even this evolved over time. I remember one routine where I used the word "crap." The word is technically a scatological phrase. But I used it all the time, and, although some people may have found it perhaps vulgar, I didn't, as it best described the meaning I was trying to convey at the time.

Anyway, I was told by an agency that booked Christian events not to use the word, as it would be offensive to some Christians. Since I make my living using words to communicate ideas, I have come to realize some words create an image or idea that best defines the mood you want to communicate, even if these words are sometimes coarser. Yet that coarseness is what gives the word its impact!

I believe Paul used this technique in Philippians, when he said he found all he gave up in this world to pursue Christ was as worthless as "dung" compared to what Christ gave him. Always the rebel, I found the elimination (no pun intended) of the word "crap" from my vocabulary to be a type of legalism that didn't afford me the right to be human to the rest of humanity. When we are told to "not eat meat" so as not to offend our brother who finds it offensive, I think it's telling to realize the Bible describes this offended brother as the weaker of the two.

Yes, we are to give our God-given rights away when those rights may offend, but we pay this price because so many Christians have allowed their immaturity and traditions to dictate the behavior of everyone else in the Body. There are some areas where our behavior needs to be corrected, but there are so many gray areas it seems to me to exemplify the fact God uses many different types of people to communicate His ideas.

The self-righteous who feel it's their duty to censor the rest of us try to mold us into the package they believe Christianity must look like, sound like, and feel like. They suppress the uniquely individual walk the Judeo/Christian God has given

His children, thus stifling the ability for these same children to reach many nonbelievers only THEY can reach!!

Immaturity is a constant theme in the New Testament and it's used to illustrate why the Church continues to stagnate and render itself ineffective in relating to the culture at large. Am I saying we should be allowed to sin in order to show the world we relate to them? NO! What I am saying is sometimes what we consider sin in the behavior of a brother just may not be sin, whether we like it or not! Of course, most of you reading this book would not consider yourself in the category of immature, so all I have to say to you is...hell, damn, ass, and piss!

"Huh?!" you are saying to yourself. Did that take you off guard, my using curse/scatological words for no reason? Take a deep breath and relax.

You have just experienced another "Brad Stine Experiment." If you were instantly offended by those words and feel violated or appalled that I would suddenly use what you perceive as sinful and inappropriate words for a Christian to ever utter, I have only one idea to share with you. Every one of those words is in the Bible! Remember our paradigm of content over context? We must train ourselves not to judge content until we decipher the context.

You may ask, "So, Brad, what was the context of using the frightening words?"

By simply using those words before I told you where they came from, I allowed you to see how quickly even "mature" Christians can jump to conclusions (usually, by the way, negative conclusions) before the evidence is weighed. The context was to prove that many judge appearances without the facts.

Let me give you a story. As I already mentioned, I worked the summer of 2003 and many years after as a platform speaker for Promise Keepers, which was a great and noble ministry I was honored and proud to be associated with. I spent that summer building trust among the staff.

As I prepared for the 2004 season, a Christian man wrote a scathing letter to Promise Keepers, telling them he saw me on Comedy Central and I was using the Lord's name in vain. He then called my management to air his grievances there. He told my manager how he saw me at Promise Keepers and bought my first DVD, *Put a Helmet On!*, and he was amazed that there I was, cursing on television. He knew it was me as the comic used the "Put a Helmet On!" line, and he could tell it was me just by watching. He also explained how he prayed for three weeks before writing a formal letter to Promise Keepers, but finally did it after consulting with others in his church, including a man in the newspaper business.

Now, I applaud anyone who stands for righteousness and is willing to hold a brother accountable for his actions; I believe we need more of that. I also applaud anyone who prays and seeks godly counsel before making a decision.

There was just one little problem: apparently God neglected to tell this man before He "released" him to slander me...

HE WAS WRONG! The comedian he saw who resembled me and had a similar line and delivery style was Denis Leary! Ironically, this sterling man of God was able to take the time to write Promise Keepers and potentially damage my relationship with them (it didn't, as they inquired of me first before rushing to judgment, which, coincidently, is the biblical model), but found it too difficult to take the same time to write me a letter of apology.

THIS is a demonstration of immaturity in action, which continues to make Christians look bad in the sight of the world. In this brother's "zeal" to point out the perceived sin in another brother, this guy ended up committing possibly five of his own: (1) "judging" before having all the facts, (2) "slander," which is illegal, (3) "gossip," (4) "schism," by bringing others into the mix who had nothing to do with the problem, thus causing them to sin, (5) not obeying the clear biblical process to which he alleges to adhere, by not approaching me first! and (6) fornication—okay, not fornication. I just threw that in because I was ticked at the guy!

But look at how easily all of this could have been avoided! Had he simply followed what the Bible commands, which is to come to me first, all would have been resolved, he would have done his duty, and everyone could have learned something. Instead, he ended up in my book.

Future slanderers beware! Next time I'm liable to name names!

Even as I write these words, I find myself angry and hurt by the actions of one guy. This is my immaturity and I need to make sure my motivation is to use this example to demonstrate how not to judge, without putting myself in the position of doing it myself and finding myself becoming disqualified.[1]

---

[1] An interesting sidenote appeared as I was writing this book. The man of whom I spoke actually did end up sending a letter to me through my management, apologizing for his offense. Now, I suppose he expects me to forgive him. Man, living this Christian life is rough! But this also brings up the dilemma constantly put in the way of Christians in the acting profession.

Probably the worst part of trying to serve God while working in a high-profile job is the fact I actually am expected to practice what I preach! I liked it better when I was less well known and could actually be a jerk and only a few people knew about it! This is the price of being in a profession where being somewhat of a "celebrity" is crucial to making a living. Of course, it also brings more heat on your life since you no longer can just blend into the Body.

"THE OSCAR GOES TO..."

ASSUMED TRUTH 7: All Christians will come to the same conclusion about what is appropriate Christian behavior.

What standard should Christian actors use in determining what roles they will portray? I remember searching this out myself when I was in acting class. Some of the roles, surprisingly enough, weren't written with a Christian worldview in mind! Some involved language and behavior I don't use in my daily life (or at least try not to). Christians really need to come up with their own version of a curse word. You know, something to say when we hit our thumb with a hammer, because I guarantee you, when something like that happens, you will verbally express your feelings! (Actually, most of the prophets' names would work well: "Zechariah! I stepped on a tack!")

I believe one of the great things about my faith is it tells me to work things out "with fear and trembling." In other words, I have the freedom to examine my life and to make choices that may seem appropriate now, although I may not find them appropriate in the future, and vice versa. For instance, I once was hired to act in a student film that called for my character to use an obscene word.

As I pondered this scenario, I reasoned I was playing a role of another person, one who was very different than me. In his world, this type of language is common. I figured if the only way we can take a role is if the character has a similar worldview, I would rarely have the opportunity to be in films.

Also, aren't we able to watch Christian shows in which the character of Jesus is played by an actor who isn't a Christian? Plus, by this logic that says Christians shouldn't play roles with "un-Christian" behavior—Christians shouldn't be allowed to play the role of Satan!

The ultimate anti-Christian!

I decided to take the role, but, interestingly enough, when I arrived to shoot it, I began to feel less comfortable with saying the foul word, since I spent my comedy career proving you could be edgy and provocative without curse words. So I began to talk to the director about possible options in the dialogue that could make the character more interesting. He listened and allowed us to shoot two takes with and without the offensive word. I don't know which take he ultimately used, but I do know the answer I was seeking was slowly revealed to me.

It wasn't so much the word anymore as the whole picture. Did I believe in and agree with the story of this film? As I began to examine it, I realized I did not. As a result, I knew my decisions when considering a role in film in the future would be based on whether the film would leave the audience, and consequently my culture, with a positive, meaningful message I could believe in.

In other words, I would judge the movie on context rather content. Sound familiar? Almost like a "practice what you preach" scenario! Also, being around fellow actors who were nonbelievers was an important opportunity for me to be a witness, and, by being good at my craft without compromising the real Brad, I was a witness someone may need. This was a moment in my walk where I reached a conclusion about my faith I believe was God-ordained.

I was allowed to "do it wrong" in order to discover what was right. Sometimes we judge others on where they are now, when they may very well be in the middle of a journey leading them somewhere else. I thank God my religion allows me the grace to grow. Many times I will make mistakes, but as long as my heart desires to follow exactly where God wants me, I will find the truth and that truth will set me free.

God doesn't allow difficult things to happen to you to toy with you. He doesn't allow it to tempt you or trap you. He does it to TRAIN you! Though my experience in the acting field has been nominal, there are Christians who have taken it to a higher level—those who are committed to acting without compromising their beliefs.

I remember working a church in Las Vegas once (a church in Vegas sounds as foreign as a casino in Branson!). I was performing a concert with the former group 4Him, made up of great guys I always enjoyed hanging with. In the green room, I noticed the guys talking to a man who looked somewhat familiar to me. I asked him if we had met and he politely said he didn't think so. The 4Him guys started going on and on about how he was some well-known actor who was in a ton of movies. I rarely go to movies, so he didn't look familiar to me. I figured they were just messing with me, so I let it go.

That night, Jim (the alleged "actor") and his wife watched my set and the 4Him concert. Afterward, I saw him in the casino and he waved me over to talk. He was most gracious and told me how much he loved my show. Wanting to reciprocate, I told him I was sorry for not recognizing him. He and I talked about our art and about our faith.

You see, Jim was a professional actor, but he was also a follower of Jesus. Here was a man who had a morals clause in his contract; he refused to do nude scenes, as well as certain other actions that would compromise his faith and his marital relationship. Hollywood is none too keen on actors who set their own personal standards on a movie set, but this was not a place of compromise for Jim. He chose roles he felt either represented a character he believed in or a movie whose theme represented something he could stand behind.

Trying to be kind, I asked him if there were any movies coming out I could see him in. He told me there was one coming out soon called *The Count of Monte Cristo*. This is where I decided to look as stupid as I could in front of Jim; I asked him who the lead was in the film. He simply told me, without a hint of ego and almost apologetically, the lead in the film was...him.

Here we were, two artists in different fields, one fairly famous at the time, and me, a relative nobody. Yet we both respected each other's gift and place at the table in the entertainment industry. Little did either of us realize then that in only a couple of years, Jim would have the privilege of playing a character he could completely pour his heart and soul into, literally.

We were both Christians and very soon I, along with millions of other people, had the privilege of watching Jim portray the person who is the essence of both our lives. This wonderful brother took his God-given gift to portray Jesus to the world.

You see, this actor's name is Jim Caviezel and he portrayed Jesus in *The Passion of the Christ*, directed by Mel Gibson, a controversial "Christian" movie that is the most widely watched and largest grossing "religious" film in history. Had Jim not committed himself to being the best he could be in the acting profession, he never would have been considered for that role. I also believe God honored his integrity and prepared him not only as an actor but as a sincere Catholic believer.

Once again we are brought back to the truth that God has a plan for Jim's life. A plan I am sure some Christians found inappropriate because of some movies he was in before *The Passion*. What I am also completely sure of is this man is going to be around a long time in the acting profession. He will receive accolades for his skill and rewards for his commitment. He will also lay them all down someday at the feet of the One who has entrusted him with this talent.

This is what is possible for those who are completely sold out to the living God. They will know their purpose and they will watch it come to fruition in their lives as well as see its effect on those around them who can't ignore their authentic walk. These are believers who are driven by the Holy Spirit's lead in their lives, not by the expectations of other Christians. These are the ones whose insistence on being true to their faith also means being true to their mission field. Jim Caviezel's mission field is Hollywood and, guess what, he got so good they couldn't ignore him. Blessingsonya, brother, blessingsonya!

BLESS THIS HOLY HAIRDO

ASSUMED TRUTH 8: Sinners are
worse people than I am.

Many of the ideas I have been discussing in this book revolve around two main points I believe hurt not only our individual walk with God but, more importantly, our individual witness for God. One of those behaviors is the habit of emphasizing content over context. This concept shocks a lot of Christians, especially when you lay the truth right at their feet. But our fellow believers aren't the only ones guilty of this and they certainly aren't the only ones who dislike having the truth waved in their faces.

However, if sinners hate what you have to say because it is the truth, you shouldn't be surprised. After all, Jesus warned us this would happen. As he promised, this is because truth brings with it demands on people's choices, which are directly tied to the human emotion driving most human decisions—pride.

Pride is the greatest sin because it demands its own way despite what God said is allowed. Pride is original sin and nothing has changed in the intervening years to indicate things are or ever will get any better. Just as it is impossible to keep people from hating the truth you bring (John 15:18), which they will associate with you, it is imperative your aim is to continue loving them, in the hope they will begin to see in you someone they are attracted to. You may be in the process of changing their mind about who a Christian is supposed to be!

Remember: for many people the only glimpse of Christianity they get comes in the form of Christian television. They say you only get one chance to make a first impression. Some of the first Christian television I ever saw was when I was a kid in Southern California. I started watching TBN in the '70s when it launched in Santa Ana. At that time the founders looked somewhat similar to people I saw on the streets. Over time that image began to change, especially in the female hosts' looks. The overabundance of makeup style could be a little disconcerting for anyone trying to decide exactly what "look" Christians are shooting for.

This puts a whole new spin on 2 Corinthians 5:17: "Therefore if any man be in Christ, he is a new creature" ("creature" being the operative word). Of course, God said He would confound the wise with His ways, and maybe this is one of those ways we aren't supposed to understand. The older TBN always was an enigma to me. The gaudiness just didn't set well with me. Listen, folks, when your set design is such that Liberace would be saying, "Uh, it's a little much," you may want to consider toning it down.

But this also gives me a chance to examine my own prejudices. If I take a moment to think about it, I'll bet, over the years, thousands of people came across that station and stopped there simply for a laugh! It actually became their entertainment by mocking it! In the course of these episodes, they unknowingly were hearing the Gospel! Many of them,

I'm sure, also became believers from the fact God's Word never returns void. Perhaps the very fact the show's hosts appeared so unusual looking was the very tool God used to compel nonbelievers to watch a Christian broadcast! "My ways are not your ways, sayeth the Lord."

Even though some programming on TBN was weird to me, there have also been some wonderful speakers I've seen over the years on the station who I've received great encouragement from. Truth be told, if I want Christians to accept the "unorthodox" way I communicate, I have to give the same absolution to Christians I find unusual. It would seem this is really where my own judgment of fellow Christians becomes so damaging, when I ridicule those who don't do it like ME!

Yet that is the very issue I have with those who don't like my approach. Outside of blatant heresy, I'm commanded to love my brethren as PROOF I'm a believer! I don't fully grasp God's ways, but, then again, I don't often find Him seeking out my counsel. My job is to pray for those who I know are followers of the living God. I mean, wasn't it one of the same soldiers who mocked Jesus for entertainment, who, only a few hours later, proclaimed, "Certainly this was a righteous man."

When I come across spiritual dilemmas I am unable to decipher, I'm constantly looking to the life of Jesus for help. For example, I find it interesting Jesus said the world would hate us as they hated Him. I always associated the term "world" with nonbelievers, but if you look at the Gospels, something interesting emerges. Jesus was loved by many sinners. Most of the animosity and hatred for Him came from the religious sector! Is it possible when Jesus referred to "the world," He was, in many ways, referring to the religious folks who take up room in the church, but who are so steeped in their traditions they hate anyone who doesn't behave in the "Christianly" manner they demand from the rest of us?

This is the theme that has driven my walk, my career, and this book. I believe sometimes the Church has brought persecution upon itself in many ways because of its inability to "be Jesus" to the world. For instance, we are constantly taking up arms in the battle for our cultural religious heritage, which happens to be Judeo/Christian—and we should. My problem comes when Christians start singling out certain groups as seemingly more in sin than the rest of us!

The homosexual rights movement is the first to come to mind. I remember vividly the campaign to get gay marriage legalized. Part of what makes marriage important to society is it is supposed to create a scenario that builds character in the individual—character built on the expectation that when two people say they are committing their life to each other, they actually mean it!

Marriage at one time in this country actually had a holy significance, since two people were entering a covenant with themselves and God. It was performed in a church to remind people of this significance and witnesses were invited, not so you would have a better shot at getting the blender you always wanted but so they would see your covenant to each other before God and would, as a society, hold you accountable for keeping it. I'm married, so I know I don't need to tell those who are as well it's hard! Real hard! But hard is good! Anything difficult to accomplish is worth more when you get there.

I am a guy, so my partner is, of course, a woman. I say "of course" even though, for most of human existence, marrying the opposite sex was pretty much a given.

Marrying the same sex just doesn't impress me. Guys want to marry guys? COWARDS! You know why? Because anyone could marry the same sex; that would be too easy! Half the fights men and women get into would instantly vanish if we were all married to the same gender. If I married a guy, I would never have to ask where the underwear I wore yesterday are. You know why? Because it would be exactly where I threw it the night before, in the corner next to my sock!

You see, as guys, that is where we would agree dirty clothes belong, wherever they happen to end up. Not only would a guy know it was there, he wouldn't care if I wore it a couple of days in a row! Why? BECAUSE HE'S A GUY!! Guys see things differently than girls. Now, because I am a comic, I am somewhat of (dare I say the dreaded word?) a celebrity. I find myself having to be conscientious of something I never thought would be my responsibility. I actually now have to be aware of my appearance!

I recently did a men's retreat in the mountains where the lodging didn't have the same amenities as most hotels. I actually found myself in the awkward and unenviable position of having to ask for two things no guy should ever have to ask from another: an iron and a blow-dryer! My wife simply insists I keep my clothes well pressed, which is still dumbfounding to me, especially considering it was a men's event. Look, it's just guys; even if my clothes were wrinkled, they wouldn't even notice! Better yet, if they noticed, they wouldn't care!! That's the beauty of being a man! Ladies, let us revel in it.

Guys also know things girls don't. We don't judge the cleanliness of clothes on how they look, but more importantly how they smell! It's the same test you use when judging the freshness of salsa—as long as it smells right, it's edible. Your eyes simply let you know you need to remove the green stuff that has grown there since the last time you ate it. Of course, the most effective test for food spoilage is simply to give some to your friend to eat without telling him you're not sure if it's safe. If, after a few minutes, there are no abdominal cramps and projectile vomiting, it's time to dig in! Life being married to a man would be boring. You want a challenge in your life? Marry the opposite sex; now that's hard!

We have become completely Epicurean in our culture. The only gauge we use to make our next decision is, "Does it make me feel good?" All we care about is not being disturbed. But, as a Christian, our very lives are a disturbance to everyone else. Always keep in mind, Jesus said they hated Him first. Why? Because He spoke the Truth!

So what's everybody mad at me for? Remember, I didn't say I was the Truth. JESUS SAID HE WAS! I didn't say my belief system is the only way to the Father. JESUS SAID HIS WAS! I didn't say those who believe in other religions or philosophies or in no religion at all are going to Hell. JESUS DID! All I did was believe Jesus when He said it. I am a follower of Jesus; consequently, I have no choice but to do as directed by Him. I am true to my worldview.

You would think people would honor and respect that, even if they disagreed with me. The fact that they don't reveals the awful truth of humanity. Nobody is truly tolerant of others' beliefs—and they shouldn't be! Why?

Because some beliefs are antithetical to others! Absolute tolerance is impossible for anyone unless of course you believe in nothing. If nothing is absolutely true to you, then all beliefs are equal; that is, they are equally true or false, depending on your point of view. The problem with believing this way is it has the nasty habit of coming back and biting you in the hindquarters! For instance, if you're a complete pacifist and absolutely tolerant of all other beliefs and my belief tells me I can kill people who believe like you, then to be consistent with your belief, you would have to let me. My guess is that ain't gonna happen. Thus proving you don't really believe in absolute tolerance after all.

Now, back to the homosexuals and their "right" to marry. (Some segue, huh? My editor tells me I have enough tangents in this chapter to start my own geometry textbook.) When this issue was being debated a few years ago, I thought long and hard on this issue and it caused me a lot of grief. Let me tell you why. First of all, I seem to have an "artist's" way of looking at life in many cases. What I mean by that is God has gifted (cursed?) me with the notion of finding the unorthodox in life often more appealing than the mainstream.

Being in the entertainment business, I have had many gay friends. I lost a cousin to AIDS in the '80s, and I have had family members who are gay and they are some of the kindest, most generous people I have ever known and I love them. Most gay people in general I have met are some of the most interesting, funny, and creative people I have ever known. In other words, I am fond of most gays with whom I have become close.

But, once again, this is exactly what makes Christianity such an amazing Truth. We are commanded and expected to have relationships with and to love people who we believe God has told us are behaving in sin. I don't have a problem with that. I want to teach my children to stand strong for what they believe to be true. That means they will know many people in their lifetime who despise what they hold most dear.

Welcome to the real world! Many times, that comes with the price of having people hate you.

What I don't want to teach my kids is to ever believe their belief makes them superior to others. I have been saved by God, as much as I hate to admit it, IN SPITE OF MYSELF! The fact God chose me is supposed to bring me to my knees daily, not, as it often comes across, hold myself higher than others. Remember, as Christians, we are forbidden to hate any person, although we are commanded to hate any idea contrary to God's Word.

Okay, I think another Brad Stine test is in order. I remember seeing a bunch of kids once walking around with that cocky attitude thing only a teenager can pull off. The kind that makes you totally want to slap the snot out of 'em. They had all the goods, with the pants falling halfway off their hind end, and the wool beanie, even though it was August. I looked at these kids and just felt disgusted by their lack of respect for adults, their loud, obnoxious mannerisms, and just about anything else I could hate at the moment. I was never like that! How could I be? When I was their age, Barry Manilow was popular!

Then something occurred to me. My first response to these obnoxious kids (and they were) was a habit. I had a habit of first-response attitude toward anyone whose lifestyle, ideology, demeanor, and even politics were antithetical to mine. In my self-righteousness, I suddenly realized this was completely opposite from what my first response to sinners is supposed to be.

You see, part of my journey as a Christian is to be constantly "working out my salvation with fear and trembling." I need to be sober and diligent, constantly aware of how I am perceived by the secular world—not compromising my belief to make them like me, but also not trying to coerce moral behavior through arrogance and a superior attitude. The phrase "What Would Jesus Do?" was popular a few years back. I think there should have been different phrasing of the term that would really be more helpful to most of us. It would be, "What DID Jesus Do?" because we actually have a record of what our Savior did in scenarios we often find ourselves in.

What was His first response to being confronted with sinners? This is of vital importance because I am supposed to be in the process of conforming my behavior to His. Of course, His first response was—cue the trumpets here—COMPASSION! He felt sorry for these people because he saw their behavior, lifestyle, and worldview for what they were, the need for relationships they did not possess.

This is what was missing in my life as well. I needed to see the unlovely not as people who are destroying "my" culture but as people who are likewise being destroyed by a culture that has refused to establish absolute moral boundaries. What every homosexual, unruly teenager, anti- Christian bigot, and amoral ideologue needs is exactly what I need and needed—to know my life has meaning, to know someone somewhere will love me, to believe I am significant to somebody.

Of course, the only Being who can truly fill that void is the very one we let go of a long time ago: God. Although God is the ultimate answer to completed relationship, He uses human relationships to give us that sense of uniqueness we all crave. I mean, God loves me completely. He is the only Being who will love me no matter what I do or what decisions I make. He loves me individually in that He said He knows even the number of hairs on my head. He will never leave me or forsake me—but He doesn't love me more than He loves you. He can't!

That is what makes God who He is. He is no respecter of persons. As badly as I want to believe God absolutely can't go on without me, I am deluding myself. God doesn't need me. I need Him. He wants me, but He wants every created soul to inhabit His kingdom, even though He knows all too well most will not. That is the great heartache of the living God. He has saved me and has asked me if I would please represent Him in such a way on Earth that I could compel more of His lost children to come home.

Because God loves all equally, He doesn't love any of us more than the others and how glad I am of that! I don't get a superior place in His kingdom, only an equal one with the rest of the unworthy. I want special status though. I want the Lord to be especially mindful of me and the incredible sacrifice I make to live for Him and conform to His image. If I'm not diligent, it's easy to think that somehow God should have a little extra love and mercy set aside for me, being as I am so holy and all. Thank God, He doesn't.

I remember once hearing a celebrity actress lambasting my people over a pro-life stance they took and I wanted to ridicule and denounce her. Ironically, this was a young lady who came from the church I attended in Franklin, Tennessee, and went on to great fame in Hollywood. She went there with the lofty goal of representing Christ to that dark enclave of America, and her and her family were baptized together before setting out on this new career journey. She not only achieved the stardom she sought but along the way didn't just walk away from her faith but seemingly became antagonistic to it and morphed into the very antithesis of what it represents.

She literally became an enemy to my people and my Lord. My first inclination when hearing one of her many diatribes was to fight back in anger and revenge toward her and her lofty position she uses to demean, mock, and censor my people and our religious liberties. It was then I heard the Lord speak softly to me like a grieving father. He said, "If you ever run into my daughter someday, could you tell her I love her and I miss her and long for her to come home? She has lost her way and is destroying the beautiful life I intended her to have. I miss her."

It was startling to hear but humbling to remember I can't un-earn God's love but He will always leave the ninety-nine to shepherd back the wanderer. We all experience pain and loss throughout our lives. We cry out to God through the years longing to be given a special, unique, and personal experience with the Father.

Here's the beautiful truth. I do get to experience having that superior place on Earth. One of the greatest revelations I have received so far in my life is the unique love I crave, the special love I have hoped for, the selfish love that asks if there is anyone who will love me more than anyone else in the whole world does exist. She comes in the form of my wife.

This is the way, I believe, God is able to manifest to each of us that one-of-a-kind love: in the bond of marriage. That is why marriage has always been male/female, because we come from each other, are similar to each other, and yet are so totally different from each other we are able to fill in the missing pieces in one another in a way only the opposite gender possesses.

This is why heterosexual marriage is so important and sacred to God. He gave each of us equally half of the whole human, which literally "become one" physically, emotionally, and spiritually when those two separate entities decide to merge with each other and live the covenant they promised to God, their family, and society when they said, "Till death do us part."

There is absolutely no more important relationship on Earth than that which was the model for humanity: two separate and distinct humans coming together to form one flesh, which in turn creates a new flesh-child who is neither the mother nor the father but is half of each, making them an equal whole to the family. This is the "Trinity" demonstrated in the human situation. That is why God is very serious when He says, "I expect you to get married and stay married."

But the heterosexual world has dropped the ball on that plan, haven't they? Worse yet, Christians have joined them. This is why I didn't understand why our most vocal emphasis was aimed at saving marriage by going after a group of people who have done the least up to that point to destroy it. Why have we chosen this one group and demonized them for being the main cause of the destruction of the family?

Now, please don't misunderstand me: I think it's obvious anyone who believes a child isn't better off in a family with one mother and one father who are committed to each other for life has truly reached the pinnacle of narcissism. Obviously, thousands of years of recorded human history have pretty much established this formula as the best for society.

And that is really the issue. Just because people have done it wrong by dishonoring this God-given institution does not mean we shouldn't keep our standards at the highest level. But who are the people who have done it wrong the most? I mean, we all sin. Yet, when it comes to the destruction of the family, no one has come closer to destroying it than the HETEROSEXUAL!

As Christians, we should be the most ashamed. Just look at our own track record! We are not only supposed to set the standard for morality in society, but God has also given us the unenviable task of actually having to live it! Is homosexual behavior sin in the eyes of the Judeo/Christian God? Of course! I didn't write it; God did. Are we as Christians supposed to speak out against sin when we see it? Yes!

But what is usually missing in these scenarios of accusation is compassion. Once again, "What DID Jesus Do?" Whenever Jesus encountered sinners (who weren't of the religious persuasion), the first thing He seemed to do was create a relationship of trust with them.

Remember the woman we spoke of earlier who was behaving in inappropriately sexual ways. (By the way, any sexual behavior outside of marriage God finds equally offensive.) Here is a chance for Christians to observe a real-life scenario where God is responding to an actual case of someone in actual sin. It is at this moment when Jesus makes one of the most provocative and famous statements ever to come out of Christendom. This statement seems to sum up everything God is to man and what man is to be to his fellow man.

Jesus said, "He that is without sin among you, let him first cast a stone at her." Notice Jesus is not denying the woman has sinned, but He seems to be putting into place a template for Christians throughout the ages. Sin is real and it needs to be confronted and ceased, and it starts in your own life first!

I can understand Christians rising to confront those who would try to base the standards of the day on personal desires. The Epicurean model that started so long ago has firmly rooted itself into the hedonism of modern America. My wants and my desires take precedence over everything else. But what has created the environment that would even allow our culture to entertain the idea of legal abortion and homosexual marriage? The sixties' sexual revolution which opened the doors on this moral morass was instigated by heterosexuals.

We started getting divorced at the same rate as we were getting married, and equally pathetic, we removed the social stigma that went along with it. We started having unmarried sex at younger and younger ages, without a sense of shame, and we began to market this lifestyle to sell music and other products to our kids!

We started having abortions at an alarming rate, claiming humans have the right to sex but no obligation to take the responsibility that goes with it. Heterosexual men for years have gotten women pregnant and just abandoned them to fend for themselves, and since the sixties, women have proclaimed they want the right to be as pathetic as men when it comes to recreationalizing sex, instead of seeing it as a literally holy union of committed married partners.

We are the ones who started living together in a formerly "marriage only"-type habitation. We are the ones who once defined pregnancy as a miracle, whereas now it's a mistake.

Heterosexuals basically told the culture at large marriage and family are not what they used to be or even what you want them to be—but it is none of your business! Worse yet, statistically, people who call themselves Christians get divorced at the same rate and by some statistics a HIGHER rate than non-Christians. We are having sex outside of marriage too. We are having abortions.

We are abusing the grace of God. When the world looks to us for proof that morality is absolute and, more importantly, can be lived out day to day in the real world, this is what they see! Once the majority (heterosexual) told the culture we don't even value "old-fashioned family values," why wouldn't homosexuals say, "If the marriage concept can be whatever you want, why can't we jump in too?"

Granted, the gay marriage concept needed to be vigorously addressed, as it was trying to create something new: a "right" never even considered before. I understand the passion of those who consider it detrimental to a society that already has a skewed view of traditional marriage and I agree with their zeal. What I am equally concerned about, however, is the perception that Christians hate gays. I don't and if that is how we're perceived, we're doing it wrong!

I don't want gays to have marriage rights given to them simply because they are cohabiting, but I don't want marriage rights given to heterosexuals who are cohabiting either and we did it first! If legal rights are given to cohabiting heteros who aren't married, isn't it obvious gays would demand the same rights? In other words, gay Americans came to realize WE changed the rules and opened Pandora's box, which has relegated marriage as essentially a hedonistic free-for-all that takes the shape of whatever "scene" you're into.

THIS IS MY POINT! We sit here wringing our hands at the 1 percent of the population who call themselves gay, while we have watched the heterosexual majority truly redefine family and create the environment that has destroyed who we were. We've watched and done nothing while the floodgates have opened to a world where "family" is meaningless. I only have so much time on this earth. I have to choose my battles wisely. I have been chosen to be a missionary.

All Christians are called to be witnesses to the uttermost parts of the earth. I was chosen by God to have the U.S. as my mission field. I have also chosen to spend the majority of my moral outrage directed toward the one group I actually understand: heterosexuals, in particular, Christian heterosexuals.

You see, I have firsthand knowledge of the damage divorce creates in the psyche of a child because I am a child of divorce. Anyone who would argue that the BEST possible scenario for a child isn't a mom and a dad, committed in marriage for life, is so completely self-absorbed and narcissistic it boggles my mind. Not to mention this concept of choosing to have a child without a father because there are women who consider us unnecessary.

I can't even begin to imagine what this new breed of children will feel like when they discover their father will never be known to them because they are a result of a "choice" their mother made to have them from a test tube. This is why Christians must once and for all determine that marriage is holy and immutable and cannot be severed. We must acknowledge our sin and repent for what we as divorced believers have done to our own families and culture.

If we would make it our priority to get Christian parents to stay together and to pass our ideals about marriage and family on to their kids, maybe we could actually demonstrate that what we believe is better, instead of talking about it as if it's a theory. If we could put our financial resources to creating free counseling and/or workshops which we demand the engaged couples in our church attend, so we can really demonstrate how hard this is gonna be, then maybe we could train them on how to stay together or even persuade the "not ready" to wait.

Maybe teams from our churches could be created to mentor those whose marriages are on shaky ground, going to their homes if necessary, as we see the shaky marriage as a mission field and our calling. Maybe it's time to take a new long look at how we respond to those in our churches who are in the process of getting divorced and perhaps even take the radical position of vehemently denouncing their decision as, gee, let me think, A SIN!!

Then maybe, just maybe, we could change society from the inside out by creating a family atmosphere the world envies and is drawn to. You see, guys, it appears a little muddled to proclaim the sanctity of marriage as our top priority, then have only 50 percent of Christian marriages to point to as proof of our commitment.

There are many areas of the Christian experience I do not understand. But the one thing I do know is Jesus has been for me a sanctuary from the fact my life is not everything it should be and it never will be. "What Did Jesus Do?" is my model for trying to make the hard decisions. I simply want to offer Jesus to anyone and everyone who doesn't know life can have meaning because that is what changed my life.

But more often than not this ideal comes in the package of arrogance not unlike that of a former lifetime smoker. It seems people who finally break free from a habit, whether it is smoking, drinking, gambling, or whatever, are oftentimes the least tolerant toward those who are still engaging in these practices. You would think those who went through this trauma would be the best equipped to bring compassion to those still trapped.

I saw this same scenario play out in my own life. The first time I laid eyes on my future wife, I was smitten. She came walking past me with this amazing, wild, thick hair pulled up on her head. She was wearing clothes that made it impossible not to notice she came in the form of the female persuasion. You see, this was a woman who went through relationships that were no longer fulfilling. She prayed to God He would show her what to do in order to live the life He wanted for her. This was also a time in my life where I was coming off the tail end of a prodigal journey I was on for maybe ten years. Consequently, the timing was right for both of us.

The interesting thing about being on a prodigal journey is you can never really enjoy it. You know your Father, you know your family, and yet you choose to disregard them so you can indulge in the best Satan has to offer. Once I regained my senses, an event that always seems to come to you in the middle of a pigpen, I was ready to repent and commit to the Truth I knew all along.

Once I met my future wife, I found out quickly she was a believer in Jesus. This came by way of an early childhood experience of being raised Catholic. But what was even more interesting was she was completely committed to the ideas of New Age teachings. She believed in reincarnation, all religions are true, and she was a devoted follower of the system of revelation in the form of astrology.

This was the woman God planned as His gift to His wayward follower. The first thing anyone in my position has to do is get that girl to church! Even in my fallen condition, I was able to discern she was in much more need of repentance than I was (wink, wink). I took her to church, where she committed herself to Christ at the first service we attended.

From that point on, I felt my mission was to demand she completely abandon her New Age beliefs because they were contrary to the teaching of the Bible. Interesting how passionate I was to make sure she instantly conformed her thinking to God, when I took years to indulge my flesh, all the while shaming Christ and abusing His grace.

Such is the act of the "religious" mind, which always finds others' sins more heinous than his own. I remember getting in huge fights over these issues and found myself exasperated by her inability to immediately see her Christian walk the way I did. But God was gracious and gave me a life lesson I have never forgotten.

As a comic, I was constantly traveling and I noticed when I was gone, Desiree continued to go to church. My point is she was drawn to the Truth and by her fruit was demonstrating outwardly what happened to her inwardly; she was indeed a new creature. She was a true follower of Jesus. I say that only because God allowed me to reason with Him.

I simply asked myself, "Is she saved?" The answer was yes. Then I thought, "Well, that means she has the same Holy Spirit I do, right?" Yes is the obvious answer. So, said I, if that is true, then perhaps as she continues to study the Word of God and fellowship amongst fellow believers, she will begin to change habits and characteristics that defined her in the past as the Holy Spirit works in her individual walk.

I was going to take the radical position that maybe God could guide her better than I could and perhaps I needed to trust He always loves our loved ones even more than we do. After all, they were His first. So instead of demanding, I discussed things with her, and when she occasionally brought up something related to her New Age beliefs, I just let it go.

I loved her and trusted God would change her heart in His time. Over time she talked of it less and less, and eventually admitted it no longer was something she believed God wanted her to be involved with. It happened organically, almost as though God knew what He was doing!

But I didn't change her! God did. I came to realize I was judging her where she was in her walk instead of where she was headed in her walk.

This is why judging a fellow believer is so arrogant and sinful in the eyes of God. We are judging people based on information we don't possess. If I tell my wife I'm going to the store, I don't want her being angry at me because I'm at a stoplight. I'm on the way; I'm just not there yet!

The one thing I am sure of, being privy to the Christian worldview, is all humans are seeking a relationship with God, because it is the severing of that relationship at the Fall that has perpetuated every painful thing that has come to the human race since! As Christians, we are the light bearers of a forgotten time when there was an Eden. It was our first home and we have spent our entire lives trying to return there. Problem is, it isn't here anymore. But its residue resides in the empty place in our hearts longing for fulfillment. It is this human experience we as believers share with every human on Earth.

The answer to this dilemma has been established in the form of the God-man named Jesus. If we, who have the most to be grateful for, find ourselves investing more time in signing petitions to let Congress know we are against gay marriage or we are for Ten Commandments monuments in government buildings than we do seeking out, befriending, and building loving, sincere relationships with these people, then it occurs to me we are living a life where our first response is anger instead of compassion, hate instead of love, and arrogance instead of humility. That is definitely not "What Jesus did"!

"MY BRAIN HURTS!"

ASSUMED TRUTH 9: Once you're
saved, you never doubt your faith.

I'm a founding fathers fan. Everything about them blows me away. They created the opportunity for our lineage to break away from the most powerful country of their time and start our own country based on a constitutional republic. They were intelligent visionaries and dreamers. Heck, I'm even impressed by their penmanship! Think of it! They wrote one of the most important documents in human history on parchment with a bottle of ink and a feather, all by candlelight no less! If you give me a lined legal pad and a five-hundred-dollar Montblanc pen, I'm still going to write outside the lines!

I believe the United States of America, though flawed (kinda the price a country pays for being run by people), is the greatest country that has ever existed on Earth. Some people from other countries would call that an arrogant statement, but I don't. I think it's fairly easy to decipher whether a country is great or not. Do people want in or do they want out? And I don't know of any country people want in more than the U.S.! Rarely do I run across articles in the paper telling about the hundreds of aliens stuffed into a boxcar trying to sneak their way into North Korea!

I don't read a lot about people hiring a "mule" to smuggle them into Communist China! All countries run by atheistic ideologies or religious philosophies that don't allow dissent are oppressive, and oppressive countries don't bode well in attracting immigration. Why do you think the former Soviet Union finally dismantled when the best slogan the chamber of commerce could come up with was "Come to Russia; we'll give you a turnip"!? This is why liberals who constantly look to Europe for guidance confuse me! "Look at the European model," they cry, or, "We can learn a lesson from our European allies." Blah…blah…blah. I'm always like, "Hey! We left Europe—on purpose! And you know what we've got? The United States of America!

You know what they've got? FRANCE!!" I rest my case.

France has become the international punch line but they're not alone. Europe in general has abandoned the Christian ethos that established it for so long, and we have and will continue to watch in real time what the end of a great civilization looks like when it abandons its history and traditions—and especially God. Yet, I can't hate them. Not because I don't want to—that is one of the many downsides to Christianity.

My religion forbids me to hate people. Oh, I want to hate people, but God won't let me. This is another example of what makes Christianity so great: it demands you behave differently than your flesh desires. So I simply have to resort to remembering the sage advice my grandmother used to give me in the form of a cliché, which was, and I quote, "If you can't say something nice"—about an overrated, ungrateful

European nation that would have been wiped off the face of the earth twice in the twentieth century if it weren't for the United States and has given nothing meaningful to the culture in the last two hundred years but wine and cheese, both of which are made better in California—"then don't say anything at all"!! And I live by that!

Of course, France has always marched to a different drummer. Let us not forget, these are the people who gave us Voltaire. When I began writing this book years ago, France was preparing to outlaw the right of people to wear religious symbols of any kind in the workplace. They believe the state should always create an environment of neutrality, which, of course, always comes in the form of antireligious bigotry.

Interestingly enough, one of the definitions of religion is "a point or matter of ethics or conscience." Once again the concept of "ethics," as in "not wanting to offend others," is what's driving this neutrality effort.

So the very ethic that imposes this antireligious oppression exists because of the moral constructs of religion. This borrowed religious idea (offense) is also used by atheists to remove religion in general from public discourse. I would think if the only way your ideology can drive your point across is by having to draw ideas from an antithetical belief system, perhaps you should reevaluate your worldview!

Let me take a moment to explain my case and please bear with me, as I'm not a professional philosopher. Atheism is materialistic, meaning they believe nothing exists outside what is considered material (atoms/molecules).

They believe humans are simply an advanced formulation of molecules because we have the ability to reason. The fact they cannot account for where reason comes from is a whole other argument. The problem with this ideology is it means as a thinking species, we are an accident. There is no God; henceforth, there is no plan for us to be here. Matter, motion, and time serendipitously ended up making humans.

SO—that means all the "ethics" and rules of law we have, like being nice to each other and not running over your teacher with your car when you get a bad grade, are simply ideas or preferences we have agreed to adhere to. In other words, it's not actually wrong to steal; we have just decided to say it is.

This brings us back to being offended. We assume it matters when someone gets their feelings hurt, when, in fact, how can you hurt the feelings of a bunch of molecules? The humor in this self-delusional belief system would be funny if it weren't so tragic.

Without God, we never really know what a moral standard is, let alone if an immutable one exists. But the truth is God is not an easy concept to grasp. We have been trying to grasp Him since the beginning of time and we still find ourselves wondering if we have gotten any closer. Growing up in the church, everything about God to me was simply a given. The faith of a child is absolute. The problem is kids grow up. Santa Claus is a fantasy along with the Easter Bunny, ghosts, and the belief in man-made climate change. (Sorry, I couldn't resist.)

It was because of the perceived autonomy I possessed, revealing itself in physical and intellectual maturity, that I came to a point in my life where I needed desperately to know if God was real. It became a defining moment when I had to decide if God was a tradition or the Truth. Just reading the Bible no longer sufficed; I needed supporting evidence.

This crisis of faith came at a time when I realized playing religion or behaving in the traditions of religion was no longer enough to convince me. Yet one comfort that came my way as I began to study was the realization that just about every Christian I ever admired went through this same process!

It's almost like an initiation God puts desperate seekers through in order to prepare them for the idea of committing every part of themselves—body, soul, spirit, and mind—to Him. He demands complete surrender, including the parts of my intellect I put so much trust in. As I studied religion and its supposed antagonism to science, I discovered some very complex concepts used by the intellectual reason of materialists to disbelieve in God actually worked against them.

Because before you can disbelieve in God, you have to begin to reason, and reasoning is a process that is the ultimate argument for God's existence. Why? Because the ability to "reason," as well as the laws of logic which we must possess in order to call ourselves rational beings, comes from a place no one can find. Because the ability to reason is not found in matter, it could only come from God. (Read "The Argument from Reason" in C. S. Lewis's *Miracles* or the book *C. S. Lewis's Dangerous Idea: In Defense of the Argument from Reason* by Dr. Victor Reppert.)

For Christians who have the ability to grasp it, it will destroy all arguments the materialist has for his disbelief. It's not easy to grasp, but the things of God, as we have argued already, shouldn't be. I also started discovering many reputable scientists were, in fact, theists! Not to mention the giants of early modern science were, almost to a man, Christians. From Bacon, Copernicus, and da Vinci to Pascal, Newton, and Pasteur, science as we know it began with men such as these, and, if you're a Christian, these men, and countless more like them, are your lineage!

No wonder atheists are so antagonistic to religion in general and Christianity in particular. Their god is science; yet modern science was founded essentially by Christians. In other words, they're a little jealous! But they also seem to be jealous of the fact that somehow we, as believers, have found meaning in nature they have searched for *from* nature. We all receive the same information; we just have to interpret it differently based on what we already believe to be true about an ultimate designer.

Christians see in the intricacies of the molecule the handiwork of an intelligent designer; atheists simply see the end result of an incredibly complex (though unplanned) machine that works perfectly, and by "discovering" what was already there, they have convinced themselves they somehow invented it.

Atheists like to demean the theist with the old adage, "Religion is a crutch." My response is, "What's wrong with a crutch?" What is a crutch used for? It is used to hold you up when you can't hold yourself up. (There is no more deluded human than the one who believes he is in control). A crutch allows you to move forward when you were previously stagnating. It assists you when no one else is there to help. And, finally, it is used only until you are healed and complete! Those of us who see God simply must exist have no problem defining Him as such. After all, that is exactly what He promised He would be—the lover of His creation who promises never to leave your side until you make it home and are complete!

The truly fulfilled man acknowledges his weakness and is grateful God is there. The atheists so desperately need for God not to exist they will use the most sophisticated scientific means known to the most intelligent researchers to prove intelligence doesn't exist in the universe except in their own heads. They always have to use reason to prove our knowledge of ourselves is an unplanned accident. They find meaning in knowing what they discover is meaningless. Makes sense, doesn't it?

God has left evidence of His existence throughout our world and atheists literally have to rip out their own eyes and self-administer lobotomies not to see it. They delude themselves into not allowing their reason to see life plainly for what it is. Yes, my friend, if theism is a crutch, atheism is a coma!

But at least part of their thinking is simple human nature. It took me a lot of work and a refusal to give up on looking for God until I found Him. Because of the handicap of living only in three dimensions, we have to perceive God in subtleties. Yet, in the same brain God gave me to look for Him is the mindset that still questions His existence periodically.

I realize I am only three-dimensional and since we as humans have concluded there may be ten or twelve dimensions out there (and probably infinitely more), if God IS real, THAT'S where He lives. He, by definition being omnipresent, would exist in all dimensions simultaneously. Considering God created dimensions, He must have lived outside of them previous to the creation of matter. So, in order for the complexity of God to be dimensionalized, He had to create untold dimensions for His awesomeness to be contained within (if He is).

One of those dimensions is the third. That's where we live. So just as a two-dimensional being would be unable to see us in our natural form because it doesn't possess the senses to perceive all angles of us, God doesn't appear to us like some giant bearded man sticking his head through the sky and saying, "Ta-da!"

God says if we saw Him in our present state, we would die. I imagine this is because we wouldn't be able to handle the information, since we only have five senses, an awareness of only three dimensions, and our limited analytical reasoning to even search for the God question. It would amount to sensory overload. God realized that because of our dimensional handicap, He could only reveal Himself by completely joining the third dimension. In other words, He would have to become one of us. All of this totally made sense to me and enabled me to use my God-given reason ("LET'S REASON TOGETHER") to seek Him.

See, the more you define God by what He would have to be in order to claim the title God—He has to be all-powerful, all-knowing, and in all places at the same time—the more you realize a being like that would have to be communicated with differently than the way we do with our own beings. That's where prayer and faith come in.

Every time we pray, we have to believe something hears us and cares that we're talking. Even the nonbeliever who reaches that familiar place where he yells out, "If you're real, show me!" has reached a place where he is willing to take a risk that this could be plausible. He has taken a step of faith.

Still, faith can be very frustrating when we don't see or understand why God couldn't have made Himself even more accessible to us in the format we are used to. Then again, if He is who He would have to be to be God, then that's probably what faith actually is. We are communicating with something outside our reason and understanding. We are talking to something that not only knows the answer to everything we ask but even knew what we were going to ask before we did!

I think the reason some people struggle with the God concept is because they haven't actually taken the time to ponder how immense God would have to be. If you really believed an all-knowing, all-powerful being existed, the fact you wouldn't be able to wrap your mind around most elements about Him would be obvious! This is exactly how you would want it!

Amazingly enough, many atheists choose to not believe in God because there are so many areas about Him they can't understand. Ironically though, using what limited intellect we have, we would have to reason, if God were who we would imagine Him to be, part of what makes Him God is the fact so much of Him is intellectually unattainable.

I don't want a God I can understand! If the Creator of the universe's intellect is equal to mine, we are all in a world of hurt! The very fact I cannot wrap my mind around most aspects of God is why He gets to be called GOD!! We, on the other hand, are called people. We have difficulty believing in Him because we can't grasp Him the way we do three-dimensional figures, and yet that puts Him in the very category He has to be in to be God!

Prayer and faith seem to ask us to trust, communicate, and heed the standards of something in a way we previously have only done with tangible beings and concepts. It's as though we are asked to ignore our senses, which are all we have ever used up to this point to prove something existed. But if you see faith in God not as having your mind suddenly becoming irrational in the psychotic sense but as recognizing faith as another sense we possess and yet don't fully know how to utilize, then it suddenly becomes rational.

It's similar to our understanding of the existence of wormholes, black holes, and quarks—elements of nature we have never seen, although we have theorized their existence based on other, observable evidence. When we commit ourselves to God and trust in Him, we see our lives instantly take a shape we didn't previously know was attainable. I don't mean suddenly everything happens the way we want it to. Instead, there is peace knowing we are in the hands of the Designer, and we intuitively know we are in the perfect place, a place we were dislodged from by our disbelief. The skeptic cannot and will never understand these things because he has shut down his "sixth sense," which is faith.

Faith, by the way, is the only way this phenomenon can be experienced.

But isn't faith simply believing in something without facts? Well, let's have a parable. Pretend you are an explorer and you come across an ancient village surrounded by thick trees. You trek through them and come across a village of ancient people who have lived there for a millennium. They have fresh water, food, and a huge tree they worship as god. They have a pristine life but have only one genetic flaw: they are blind. They are not only blind, they have never seen, so they literally can't even imagine what sight would be. It's a complete mystery and impossible to create in their minds.

They come to you and welcome you, saying, "We have never had a visitor here. Please let us take you to our sacred tree."

You see the tree is quite a walk from you and say to them, "Thanks, but you don't need to, I see it."

They would be confused. "Oh, you mean you can smell the fragrance of the leaves in the morning? Yes, you have smelled our sacred tree."

"No," you say, "I don't smell it but I believe it's here since I can see it."

They can't quite understand what you are getting at, so they surmise, "Oh, someone has brought the fruit to you so you can feel the smooth texture of its skin?"

"No," you say. "No one brought me your fruit but I believe in it as I can see it."

"Oh," they say, "you can hear the leaves rustling through the wind and experience our tree that way?"

"No," you say, "I don't hear it as it is too far away but I can see it!"

Finally in frustration they say, "Oh, someone has brought you a bite of our fruit and it is so ripe that you have tasted its sweetness as the nectar runs down your chin!"

"No," you say, "I haven't tasted it or smelled it or felt it or heard it but don't worry, you don't have to convince me. I know it is real as I can see it from here."

These people would then have no choice but to respond to you, "Sir, you are a LIAR! No one can experience our tree if they haven't used at least one of the four senses God has given us."

Thus ends the parable. You see, in their world four senses is all they have ever known, so not only does sight not exist as an option, they literally can't even conceive of it. Yet you know something they don't. There is a fifth sense that not only exists but gives you even more information and proof than they can conceive.

Well, my friends, THAT is what God says faith is. It is a sixth sense that lets you see God with spiritual eyes and is indescribable to those who have never experienced it and more importantly refuse to believe it even exists. We are told what faith is, by the way. Faith is the SUBSTANCE (material) of things hoped for (immaterial), the EVIDENCE (material) of things not seen (immaterial). It is a combination of the natural and the supernatural in unity. In other words, it doesn't matter how beautiful the sunset is—if you refuse to open your eyes to see it and then accuse me of being irrational for believing in it, who is truly the fool?

Nevertheless, even though God has told us this is how we have to find Him, our minds can still bring on moments of doubt. What I have come to realize is the doubt many of us experience actually is sometimes a truer faith than the faith of those who don't seem to ever doubt. I remember when my dad was dying of cancer and found himself at the final pages of his life story. He was raised in a Christian home but spent most of his life rebelling against it. The last few years found my dad returning to his faith, involving himself in church, and truly returning to the journeyed path he had strayed from so many years before.

When the news of brain cancer was given to him, he couldn't have known he had six months left to exist in this most familiar dimension. We had many conversations in that time and one that constantly came up was faith. You see, he constantly referred to my sister Dara, who essentially lived her Christian faith her entire life. She lived it in her constant service to others and her family and church. She was one of those believers who continued through her walk without falling. Her faith in her Creator God seemed never to waver. She believed what God said and that was enough for her. She seemingly never struggled with her faith but was absolutely driven by it. It was that commitment my dad would speak of, and when in anguish, he would say, "I wish I had faith like your sister."

He saw a gift of faith in someone else he simply didn't have. I say "gift of faith" because the Bible tells us some of us will be given this extraordinary amount of faith. But this implies the rest of us won't. See, those who are gifted with faith are possessed by it. It is part of their makeup. But part of the definition for faith is a belief not based on the scientific method.

Scientists have faith in their hypotheses. My contention is once someone has become convinced of his faith, then it isn't faith anymore to him; it has become truth. It doesn't necessarily prove it's true, only that this individual is convinced it is and lives his life accordingly.

But for the rest of us, faith will always be just that, a belief in something, even though some aspects of it cannot be completely understood or discovered. This is the faith of the evolutionist, whose faith in undirected complexity allows him to be unmoved by the myriad holes in the theory because he has already become devoted to its presupposition. Such people live by the faith that in time all things will be discovered, all challenges met, all discrepancies ironed out. The materialist believes, in time, we will possess all knowledge.

The Christian, however, believes, in time, the all-knowing One will possess us. It was on these ideas I tried to give my dad some comfort. He saw his doubts as a lack of faith. I believe God saw them differently. I told my dad that even though sometimes he had doubts, Jesus was truly who He said He was; my dad continued to believe in Him. Even though there were times when he felt he couldn't grasp Jesus the way he grasped me, he still relied on Him for salvation. Even though there were times when the path to God seemed hazy and unsure, he continued to march on in faith!

You see, to me, the person who decides to believe in spite of the fact there are difficulties in fully grasping the faith journey is actually living a much more faith-filled life! He is the one who cries out for the hand of the Savior through the mist and has determined that no matter what his mind may try to demand of him, he will not cease trusting his sixth sense, the intangible truth he is risking it all for. He is the one who simply says, "I believe"; the very fact we are asked by Jesus to have faith shows the lack thereof would be a common occurrence. That to me is not just true faith but faith in its purest form. It's the faith that walks forward on the water in spite of the waves.

My dad went to his grave believing in Jesus in spite of his intellect's demand for proof. I have faith his reward was the Creator of all things saying to him, "Well done."

TOILETS ARE ONLY FOR PAGANS

> ASSUMED TRUTH 10: Christians
> should never admit to the
> nonbeliever we constantly struggle
> with the same sins they do.

This is the presupposition of all literature: the author has to have faith he has something you don't, and when you realize the author has it, you will not only want it, you'll actually think you need it!

But by what gauge do I make that assessment? For the past thirty-one years, I have been a professional comedian, and the fact I have made a living doing comedy for that many years simply says people like what I say enough to spend money listening to it. Because of the high-profile clubs, companies, ministries, and the like that have hired my services, I'm assuming I'm somewhat good at something! Of course, speaking for a living is a far cry from writing, since the way a comic says things is oftentimes more humorous than what he actually says. Unfortunately, it's hard to display the way you say something on paper.

Anyone who has seen me live or has my first album, *Put a Helmet On!*, or any thereafter has an advantage in that they can imagine how what I'm writing would sound. They may even find value in the elaboration of themes I could only speak of in sound-bite terms in a one-hour comedy show. Time will tell if the rest of you find value in these pages.

Some people have asked why, since I am a Christian, I rarely refer to myself as a Christian comedian. Sometimes I use it if only to use nomenclature my people might better understand. But for the most part the reason is simple: because I'm not. The title "Christian comedian" seems to indicate your comedy is designed to bring humor to an audience comprised only of Christians, which seems selfish to me, since I'm sure there are some Scientologists out there who could also use a good laugh. It further implies that if you're not a Christian, you're not going to "get" or agree with the material. None of that applies to me because I made most of my living working in places most Christians didn't inhabit.

If any term defined me more accurately, I guess it could be "Conservative comedian," though that seems to be a malleable pigeonhole. Certainly, my faith drives my worldview and consequently colors my comedy, but so do my political views, sports preferences, hobbies, musical tastes, and the fact I'm married and have two kids. I'm not ashamed of being a Christian or of Jesus Christ, but I am ashamed oftentimes by the way He has been portrayed in our country by some people claiming to be His disciples. I am also ashamed by some of the ways Christianity has been demonstrated to an unbelieving world by some Christians, and, by the way, I would have to include myself in that group.

As I mentioned earlier, I spent many years indulging my flesh in the best the world has to offer, all the time knowing I was wrong and yet abusing the very grace God gave me to be able to call myself one of His in the first place. Throughout my life as a believer, which started at the age of nine, I have struggled with certain habits and behaviors I still wrestle with on a regular basis!

At that prodigal time in my life, people could have justifiably called me a hypocrite. I said I believed something including moral absolutes, yet my lifestyle betrayed my sincerity. If a hypocrite, however, is someone who doesn't always live up to the standard he believes in, then apparently the entire human race is in the same boat, because nobody has ever always done exactly what he or she said was the best way to behave. Remember, a hypocrite is not someone who doesn't always do what he believes; it is someone who doesn't believe what he says.

Now, I know there are people who would ask, "Who are you to tell us what we are doing is wrong since you have done the same things in your life?" But, of course, that makes no sense. If the only people who were ever allowed to hold others accountable for their behavior were people who never made mistakes, no one would ever be allowed to use their failures to try and lead others to a better place.

The most successful self-help group ever, Alcoholics Anonymous, was created by a man who suffered through addiction, found a way out, and simply wanted to pass his experience on to others in the same boat. Consequently, how much sense would it make to say, "Who do you think you are to tell me to stop drinking since you used to be an alcoholic!" Learning from our own mistakes is supposed to be one of the virtues of being human. Learning from the mistakes of others is supposed to be the human experience of wisdom.

Hypocrisy is probably one of the top three excuses nonbelievers use for not accepting the claims by Christians that they have found the Truth.

Yet what exactly is the hypocrisy they are observing? Is it that we are not perfect, or is it the fact that somewhere down the line Christians mistakenly gave the illusion that once you become a follower of Jesus, you no longer battle the same things non-Christians do?

When I look at myself compared to my non-Christian and Christian friends, I notice we all have common experiences. That is one of the reasons why I think it's crucial every guy who is serious about his faith form an accountability group. Not only does it force you to examine your actions for the past week, but it inspires you to make honorable decisions as you know you're going to have to tell your partners all the sins you messed up on in the past week, and as a guy, some of them are embarrassing to admit.

But the other reason guys need to be with guys is to commiserate the fact that women, like men, are very similar in their outlook on life, and this outlook is often so foreign to men it's probably the reason men's life expectancy is shorter! I have been married for twenty-seven years at this writing, and the first ten were spent constantly being told by my wife to put the toilet seat down. Day after day, week after week, all I ever heard was, "Put the seat down! Put the seat down!!"

I finally got up the nerve to ask her why this was so important, all the while knowing whatever the answer was, I was going to be confused. Sure enough she told me, and I quote: "If you don't put the seat down, when I go potty in the middle of the night, I'll fall in the toilet!"

Now, I'm sorry, folks, but I had a problem with that analysis. I'm like, "Wait a minute. Every time you go potty, you have to sit. Guys only sit half the time. In other words, we aren't nearly as experienced at it as girls are, and yet guys have never fallen in the toilet!! If you have to sit down every time you use the facilities and don't stop to look and see if there's a seat there, then you deserve to fall in the toilet!!" My contention is, if the toilet seat wasn't supposed to move up and down, it wouldn't have come with a hinge. It would have been made out of cement.

The point is, I don't know any guy who hasn't gone through the toilet seat philosophical treatise. See, folks, the human experience is just that—a human experience. It's common to us all, and if there is one theme best exemplifying the Christian worldview, it's the fact we all are fallen. The difference between Christians and non-Christians is when we sin, we feel sorry about it, whereas, when the pagan sins, he makes a reality television show out of it.

The truth is not everyone you ever talk to about Jesus is going to believe in Him. As a matter of fact, probably most people who ever live on Earth won't believe. Our only responsibility is to share the Good News, and then it's up to the individual's will and God's spirit. Part of that sharing, and I contend in this book it's the largest part of sharing, is living out the Good News first and building relationships with as many nonbelievers as we can in our lifetime. Because I don't care who you are or even how antagonistic someone may be to your faith; someday, somewhere they are going to need an arm around their shoulder and a comforting word that says, "I care about your pain." Cultures don't change by talking about Jesus; they change by "being Jesus."

I believe authentic Christianity should come in a transparent package. It's time to be real and vulnerable to the lost. What the world needs is Christians who are like them. In the world but not of it still means in it! Think of the perception a guy would have if, after he confesses he's addicted to pornography, he hears a Christian man say to him, "Hey, me too. I have struggled with it for years, but slowly God is freeing me from it."

Think of the impact it would have on someone's life if, after experiencing divorce, abortion, or homosexual behavior, this time the Christian confidant says, "I understand; it's my struggle too! Let me walk alongside you and lead you to the One who is showing me the way out of these places. Let's walk together, and I'll help hold you up on your journey, and, by the way, you can do the same for me."

I believe that is often the missing piece in how the church is engaging people in this season in America where holding someone accountable for their behavior is no longer noble but is considered shaming and judgmental. True enough, as a Body, no matter what cultural issue is at stake, God would not expect us to compromise, yet how we deliver the information should always be with tenderness and empathy. It should always come with a cup of water first! It should always come with oil and bandages and healing first.

BUT the question I think needs to be asked of those who claim Christian redemption but behave against God's moral teachings is simple. What are you unwilling to give up for the cause of Christ? When sin is justified and reimagined to be not only no longer sin but in fact blessed of God by claiming Christ's graciousness, you have created an idol of worship that has taken the place of the living God. It doesn't get any more dangerous than that.

I realize our battle is not against flesh and blood but against principalities, against powers, against the rulers of the darkness of this world, against spiritual wickedness in high places. We will always be hated and yet commanded to love. We will always be ridiculed but commanded to reason. They will try to marginalize us and yet we are called to encourage them.

Still, I'm looking for the rise of the neo-Christian in this country: someone who is educated in his faith and desperate for God and daily sacrifices his flesh for the sake of the lost by being real and admitting his weaknesses, yet never ceasing from moving forward in the quest, not to ever demean other religions or ideologies, but simply, by education, reason, and practice, to lift up the name of Christ.

All of this can be accomplished when the believer finally realizes Jesus isn't a philosophy or a religion. He's not a concept or a point of view. He's not a belief system or a great moral teacher. He is EXACTLY who HE said He was:

The way, the Truth, the Life—The End!

THE HOLY SPIRIT IS ACTUALLY MY FEELINGS!

ASSUMED TRUTH 11: Political correctness and Christianity can coexist!

We have now come to the last chapter of my first book. (And depending on sales, conceivably my last book!) The whole experience has been illuminating to me because I never thought I had anything to say that would be of any interest to anybody but my children, who, I have insisted, are obligated to listen to everything I say and to perceive it as knowledge that will never be accessible to them otherwise. That is, until they got to be about eight and ten and came to the conclusion they actually knew more about life than I could ever hope to.

I have been doing stand-up comedy for over thirty years. I have, over my career, worked with some of the top comedians in the U.S. I have performed on the same stages and in the same clubs as the best in the business. I have worked in front of thousands, hundreds, and two at a time, and let me tell you something, this job is NOT for the faint of heart. I have read, when polled, the number one fear humans say they have is speaking in front of an audience.

Wait a minute. The biggest fear of your life, the worst-case scenario you can imagine, the ultimate moment of anxiety and horror you can come up with is speaking words in front of people who hear them? Seriously? How myopic is your fear factor? Just off the top of my head without even trying I can come up with a handful of situations that would appear on the surface to be able to cause more angst than speaking. Speaking in front of a firing squad, I would think, could add some angst to the performance? How about waking up and discovering you're the last man on Earth and you hit the lottery on the same day?

How about a week before your wedding day you discover you've contracted leprosy and the only known cure is you're forbidden to wear white, ride in a limo, walk into a church, or get any catering deposits back for fifty years?

Nevertheless, there is something about speaking in front of a crowd of strangers or peers that causes deep-seated anxiety and discomfort in the vast majority of human beings. Is it the physical act of using your voice that so terrorizes people or simply communicating in a known language? If so, I'm not sure this holds true for deaf people then.

Do deaf keynote speakers before their speech begin to get sweaty palms and, since that's how they speak, would that be kind of like drowning? Can people who sign stutter, or mispronounce words with their fingers? What if they break their hand—do they have to hire an interpreter to interpret their interpretations? How do you show boredom and disinterest at a deaf lecture? Is there even a way to "boo" for people who can't hear?

These are the kinds of thoughts that constantly ruminate in my brain 24/7, and it helps sum up exactly why there are fewer professional comedians than there are brain surgeons. Because clearly something is severely wrong with a comedian's ability to simply live a normal life without analyzing and seeking the funny in the mundane.

Yet, isn't that what you pay for when you go see a comedian? Someone to show you funny where you never knew it existed before? I mean, if I can make you laugh talking about a piece of toast, maybe that is a gift in a kind of idiot savant/sideshow freak kind of way?

But maybe there is an even more important reason God allowed the comedian to exist? Historically, we were the ones given permission to make fun of the king and not get our heads cut off! The king actually needed us to help bring some relief from a weary and tedious day of conquering lesser kingdoms and throwing people in dungeons.

In the Bible it says laughter is like a medicine, and science has even proved laughter makes you healthier. And in doing so it has also proven in our modern age that there is apparently no shortage of taxpayer dollars available for scientists seeking and receiving grants for studying such unnecessary information. Not sure how you prove laughter equals health pragmatically, but it also begs the question: Do people without a sense of humor tend to be hypochondriacs? If so, couldn't they be prescribed nitrous oxide as a palliative?

They could even do control tests giving nitrous to one side and a placebo of helium to the other and then subjects could describe their existential feelings to each other. Heck, just listening to the helium speakers get deep and vulnerable while sounding like cartoon characters would cause the nitrous control group to burst out laughing, which would cause the helium group to acquire an even deeper amount of self-loathing and insecurity for which they could be prescribed nitrous as the cure, thus creating a control group tautology that could be studied by scientists looking for another grant to waste people's tax dollars on.

Anyway, what I'm getting at is there seems to have always been a purpose and a usefulness to comics in culture, with some of the most renowned through the years—from silent films to the age of monologues—being from America. There are too many to mention but there are a few I need to. From the '60s on there came a breed of comic who used his comedy to make social commentary at a time when culture wasn't listening that well. I'm talking about Lenny Bruce, Dick Gregory, Richard Pryor, George Carlin, and others. These guys, as crude as they were at times, were actually testing the boundaries of not only free speech but more importantly what subjects could and should be tackled in a humorous way in public.

You see, we all have presuppositions we live by. Christians have, or are supposed to have, a Christian worldview and thus interpret the world through that lens because once we land upon a worldview, it becomes our foundation for interpreting morals, ethics, and interaction between groups of people. But once your worldview has been established, it can be very difficult to hear and analyze other points of view because once you believe something is true, you kind of stake a claim to it.

Any antithetical belief system then becomes problematic and even can be seen as an enemy to our belief, and the truth is, sometimes it is! We are oftentimes unable or unwilling to examine the other person's perspective and thus lose the ability to either gather a deeper understanding of our own belief or have the courage and nobility to rethink it with the possibility of changing our mind if the other person is right.

Truth is the key word here. Christians are duty bound to speak truth at all times because Jesus claimed to actually be Truth incarnate. The battle between humans from the first day of autonomy was the battle between truth and lies. Jesus and his teachings are true; Satan and his teaching are lies. Satan's so good at lying, by the way, he has actually earned the moniker "father of lies." He was the first liar and he is the progenitor of them all.

Over the years I have occasionally had a pastor say, "We want you to perform at our church but just don't be political." I'm not sure what that means exactly. If by "political," you mean, "Don't ask folks to vote for a particular candidate," then fear not; I have never done that. If you mean, "Don't claim Christians must belong to a particular party," then, again, fear not—I NEVER HAVE AND NEVER WOULD! Believe it or not, Jesus loves everybody, including the people you can't stand!

But if by "political," you mean, "Don't speak about social issues," then I am afraid I can't give you that. Not only am I duty bound to seek to redeem culture through Christ but if you are a believer, then you are too! You are even given permission in the form of the rights given to you by your country. Remember once, when Paul was about to be beaten, he spoke to the centurion and asked him simply, "Are you allowed to beat a Roman citizen without a trial?" When the centurion answered, "No," Paul didn't say, "Well, just asking, but I will keep my mouth shut because a good Christian allows himself to be beaten unjustly to prove his ability to turn the other cheek!" NO, ACTUALLY! He said, "I AM a Roman citizen"!

In other words Paul used the law of the land to defend himself against his rights being abused. We in America have been given the First Amendment for just such a time as this to be able to supposedly speak freely our convictions within the marketplace of ideas! The first right given to us by the Founders was our right of conscience. If you ever wondered how it would be possible to subvert and steal that first freedom, it would have to be by reverse engineering what freedom of speech and thought actually is. Then get the rest of the country to submit to this new orthodoxy.

But, you may ask, wouldn't we see that coming? What could be so powerful, so blatant, and yet so devious we would willingly give up this freedom and actually convince ourselves we have done something noble? Could we possibly be that naïve or ignorant? What idea could lead even Christ followers to believe a lie so nefarious and do so with our eyes wide open and apparently our spirit severely numbed?

Well, my brothers and sisters, that would be the single most affective and cancerous lie that has gripped and recreated in its own image what many Americans now use as their grid for interpreting and behaving regarding moral and ethical behavior. I'm talking about political correctness.

For those who don't know, its foundation is Marxism, which is founded on atheism. Its god is the state, which is idolatry (a sin), and its purpose is to destroy and bury the Christian/Western ethic that has guided and informed the West for thousands of years. That's not conjecture or rhetoric; that's the agenda.

The great advantage to having a written history of so many millennia is it enables cultures to examine and draw conclusions as to why certain people at certain times did certain things they felt would certainly lead to the best possible society, of that they were certain. But what is also certain is it doesn't matter how well thought out a concept was or even speculatively how well it would work, the ones proposing it would be certain of one thing: they'd be the ones in charge of keeping it running effectively.

For some reason humans seem to neglect the obvious truth that no matter what society was created, what tribe was formed, or what religion was instigated, they all have one thing in common. They demand you be their subject, and make no mistake, the one unbending rule to all societies is somebody wants to rule.

Obviously, some forms of government can be benevolent. Clearly, the political system the Founding Fathers envisioned for America was potentially the most benevolent in history. The reason being it was the first time in human history the ruler of the nation wouldn't be a king anointed by birth, a dictator anointed by coup, or a military leader anointed by conquest. We were the first ever constitutional republic, ruled by the people, utilizing their rights given to them, we believed, by God, and enforcing them through the cooperation of elected officials who were voted into place to represent our voice and then would willingly relinquish their status to come back into society and live under the same laws they proposed and ratified.

There would still be a power structure but it would change hands peacefully every four years and no matter who was president, or in Congress or in the judiciary, they would be restrained by the Constitution and Bill of Rights that established exactly what our freedoms and responsibilities would be.

This was not only an unprecedented type of government but would be incredibly fragile to maintain because of the one concept the Founders were aware of all too well. Human beings are intrinsically, by our nature, sinful. This was a brutal reality that wasn't recognized by other political philosophies historically because the idea was given to us by a holy book that dared declare itself the Word of God.

Every element of what made America unique was based on the presupposition that there was an ultimate Lawgiver, the Ruler of humans, and we owed to Him not only our existence but our allegiance as well. Even though many of you reading this may be aware of this perspective of our founding, it is crucial I reemphasize it in order to help you better understand how drastically that idea has come into conflict with what has become the new orthodoxy of the American milieu, political correctness.

So let's start by my asking you a question. If someone asked you to define what political correctness was, what would your answer be? Some of you have never stopped to consider the question, which is a big fat shame on you since anyone whose culture uses a concept to demand citizens' behavior be in lockstep with this ideology regarding how they interact should be behooved to understand what exactly they have devoted their allegiance to, even if subconsciously.

Think of it on a micro level. If you have children, what do you spend most of your time doing once they reach the age when they realize they can make choices? It's teaching them and demanding they behave and respect your authority.

You are creating a power structure in your home. But no one considers you a despot or establishing a totalitarian regime simply because you want your children to behave, do they?

Instead, we honor and respect the obvious truth that you are older, wiser, and have settled upon a philosophy or worldview by which you expect to pass on to your progeny and teach, sometimes with great difficulty and pain, the traditions of your family, your faith, your culture, and character. As the parents of these children, you have been blessed with the enormous challenge and responsibility to act like little "gods" in that you have all the power to control and inspire and discipline your children in order to create autonomous, honorable and virtuous citizens of a society they are going to inherit and participate in.

For any of you having a conniption over the fact I used the term "gods" to describe you, keep in mind in the Judeo/Christian tradition that is exactly how God the Father sees you. That religious tradition actually was the first and only to state you and I were made in the *image* of God. We have been given many of His traits and abilities. We can think into the future, "Tomorrow I'm going to do this." We can think into the past, "Yesterday we went fishing."

You can create new ideas and use inductive and deductive reasoning to draw conclusions and speculate on new ones. You can take raw materials and make new inventions from them. "Here is sand, let's make glass!" We can create civilizations and laws by which to govern them. We can observe injustice and seek to remedy it and start armies in order to defend ourselves from those who choose to use their power and autonomy to steal ours.

But certainly the most amazing attribute of humans that puts us in the similar category as God is He gave us the ability to make people. We are literally creating out of whole cloth human beings ex nihilo (metaphorically, of course) that didn't exist until we decided they should, and they are in fact genetically made in our image. Because of that, we take "ownership" of them immediately. We tend to them, feeding them, clothing them, sheltering them, and protecting them. We allow them to usurp our sleep, our freedom, our autonomy, and our selfishness. We do our best to make decisions that will inform and educate and inspire them to become the best they can be because in the end, the greatest difficulty with being a parent is putting your heart and soul into another human being in order to create within them the ability to not need us anymore!

The ultimate final act of selflessness is sending them out on their own to pursue their own hopes and dreams even if those dreams don't necessarily conform to the ones we dreamed for them. What parents are doing is replicating the formula God patterned for us. We are giving you the right to choose how to live your life independent of ours. We hope and pray, of course, they will make good decisions and they will always yearn to keep our counsel and seek our insight when necessary to keep them on the right path, but ultimately, that will be their call.

What makes freedom and liberty so beautiful and yet so dangerous is they can be abused, neglected, and stolen. You see, every human individual eventually reaches a state where they gain power. Power to do as they please, power to make their own choices, and power to use their life benevolently or malevolently.

Now, I have gone to great lengths to explore the reality of what makes a human unique in the world but more importantly to re-remind ourselves that the concept of having or achieving power is not only normal but in fact necessary to be free. Sometimes in the context of talking politics we consider the word "power" to be an intrusion on our freedom, probably because it usually is.

Again, back to our Founders—they were so aware of the potential abuse of power by those who achieve it they even crafted into our body politic what we know as checks and balances so that as soon as one branch begins to assume and instigate ultimate power over the rest of us there is another group reeling them in. Notice I said "as soon as" because it was never an *if,* but a **when**, as to how this would all shake out. This is what makes the Judeo/Christian understanding of human nature so essential to forming a republic.

It sees the world for what it actually is, not the utopian vision some believe they can create. But more importantly it never gives an inch when evaluating what will happen when a certain group of humans anoint themselves the caretakers and the parents of the rest of us. It is simply a foregone conclusion that whoever anoints themselves smarter, wiser, and more philanthropic than us normal humans will demand we surrender our autonomy (power) to them since they know better what is best for us.

In Christian theology it is known as self-righteousness and we see it all the time in politically correct culture.

What do I mean by that? The politically correct formula is whoever accuses someone else of immoral behavior *first* suddenly exempts themselves from being held accountable to the same scrutiny. In other words, I can be intolerant of your point of view as long as I claim you are intolerant of mine **first**! I can be bigoted toward your perspective as long as I accuse you of bigotry **first**! I can be fearful and phobic of your opinion of human behavior as long as I accuse you of a phobia **first**!

It's a magic world they inhabit where they mysteriously become exempt from the societal consequences they impose on the rest of us.

In other words, they have made themselves out to be God. But what is their image? Where does the authority for political correctness come from? You can't have a philosophy without defining your terms. You have to understand the authority undergirding your proclamations so the people will know who it is exactly they are worshipping.

But wait! Isn't political correctness simply a system that tries to even the playing field for all people in a society? Especially marginalized people who are minorities and thus have no power to defend and protect themselves, not to mention having no means to champion their cause? Political correctness has been framed as a kind of societal agreed-upon politeness that makes sure no one is left out of being respected, redefining words to be more inclusive and eliminating years of disrespectful language, caricatures, and stereotypes used against the powerless.

Wouldn't Jesus approve of that? If that's what you believe political correctness is, then it has done its job! It has tapped into your belief we should treat each other with equal respect, which is a Christian concept society already *had*, and manipulated it into postulating there is no behavior or idea inherently sinful or less valuable.

Remember, we are a post-truth culture now in that even immutable "truth" as a notion has to submit to the desires and whims of the politically correct in order to wrestle control from anyone who disagrees with them.

What better, more effective way to do that than to convert average human beings who believed the modern notion which assumed that whatever can be proven true through facts, science, history, or observation would win the day? What a perfect cultural moment to usher in the secular religion we now know as political correctness. Political correctness is cultural Marxism. It was founded by "intellectuals" in Frankfurt, Germany, which became known as the Frankfurt School. Its purpose was to destroy the West and its values to implement its system of Marxism/socialism/communism by whatever name they could slip through the cracks.

How does it work, you ask? Okay, remember that Marx believed that workers were exploited and their labor was stolen from them by those who owned the businesses and used the workers to manufacture the items sold on the market at a profit. Because the bulk of the profit went to the owners, Marx considered that exploitive and unjust and believed the workers (proletariat) would eventually rise up against the bourgeoisie and take the business away from the evil owner to claim ownership themselves. Because obviously once THEY control the business, THEY will be absolutely fair and just and won't even seek or care about profit. No, they will only use the fruits of their labor to give equally to everyone in need.

Remember, whoever is in control always believes they are more philanthropic, more sensitive to the needs of others, and are never motivated by greed or selfishness. This is self-righteousness and pride, masquerading as virtue. Pride is the sin God hates most of all!

The amount of time it would take for me to go into the full backstory to the formation of political correctness is a lot more ambitious than this book ever intended to be, so I'm afraid you will have to do that research on your own dime.

But let me leave you with this ominous nugget of reality. When I did a Google search of the Frankfurt School for some further details, I noticed the sites that carried the info prefaced it with the caveat that the Frankfurt School was a conspiracy theory utilized by the Right or Conservatives to essentially miseducate the populace.

Gee, I wonder what could possibly be more expected than an ideology designed to surreptitiously destroy the West using the internet (a Western capitalist invention for disseminating information) to deny this surreptitious ideology even exists?

Some of you reading this may wonder why I would spend so much time trying to establish the roots of political correctness instead of getting on with my typical genius comedic take on the subject. It's really simple, actually. The premise that political correctness and Christianity are at odds with each other doesn't do us much good unless we can contrast and compare the religions. So let me "laymanize" for a moment to sort of cut to the chase.

Political correctness demands that you take your marching orders from the state. Jesus said to give to Caesar what is Caesar's and to God what is God's. So here's a quick question. What exactly IS God's? Oh—**everything**. Everything that is true, everything created, every immutable law, and every good thing. If the law of the land is demanding you censor your God-breathed command to express His Truths for the sake of someone's feelings, you are in sin and are worshipping an idol created by the hands of man.

Remember, every human being worships something or someone. Even atheists worship the gods they have established as ultimate truth. Science is usually the altar they worship at. They will deny that, of course, simply stating they use science to objectively observe the world and hopefully improve it. But because they are usually materialists, they have the presupposition that science is in fact the only access to reality humans possess. When you state any concept or philosophy owns all true knowledge inherently and that it will only take time for scientists to discover the latest breakthrough to let the rest of us in on what is true, you are giving science the role of God.

God is omniscient; thus He alone carries all knowledge within His mind and invented everything humans eventually discover. Materialists often behave with glee and astonishment when a new discovery is revealed, almost as though they invented it as opposed to simply revealing it. We now know from numerous sources that in even postulating from evidence an intelligent agent seems to be a more likely cause of the natural world you will find yourself fired, blackballed, and jettisoned from academia, because if there is one thing scientists demand in their never-ending quest to follow the truth wherever it leads, it's the evidence is forbidden to lead where they don't want it to go.

Materialism is the religion of the atheist and the politically correct and it has to be. Since man invented science and atheists demand science *rule* us, it must be considered sacrosanct and verboten to find any alternative perspective if for no other reason than it is much more difficult to control people who have the capability or the right for that matter to think for themselves.

The first strategy of political correctness is to criticize and deconstruct all Western ideas, starting with the notion the Judeo/Christian God exists and has left us a manual for how the world actually is, how it works, what went wrong, and how we fix it. Obviously, as Christians, we know the First Commandment is "I am the Lord your God," and the second is "Thou shall have no other God before me."

Once we believe the Bible is true, our only allegiance is to the principles it reveals and thus the state is always subjugated to the will of God. The Founding Fathers knew this to be true as they were crafting this great experiment. They told us in the Declaration of Independence we find these truths to be self-evident that all men are created equal and they are endowed by their Creator with certain inalienable rights, that among these are Life, Liberty, and the pursuit of Happiness.

How many of you knew that when they were describing what the inalienable rights of man were their first inclination was life, liberty, and **Personal Property**?! Without personal property you cannot be free. God Almighty gave us our freedom from creation. The freedom to walk with Him or not, the freedom to obey Him or not, even the freedom to not believe He is the authority over our lives and all creation.

Again, cultural Marxism is the **control** of property and behavior by government intrusion. To be beholden to God means you are not controllable by the government—a government, I might add, grounded in a philosophy so demeaning and self-righteous as to believe you are too fragile and oblivious to systematic oppression; they will have to weed out the dissenters for you. They will even go so far as to get offended for those who are too oblivious to realize they are being marginalized and leverage that to stifle and control those whose ideas they abhor.

Because Christianity teaches to love your neighbor, to be a good Samaritan, and to have mercy on the poor and downtrodden, political correctness harnessed that beautiful altruistic expectation and simply redirected it toward the groups it has deemed worthy. They will shame you and publicly humiliate you in the process to demand your obedience in the American church, which is so weak and so unwilling to sacrifice whatever God would ask for the sake of Truth that we willingly comply. We literally give away our God-given freedoms and rights for a political system antagonistic to our faith in order to keep from being made to look or FEEL unloving.

In other words we trade our sacred treasure for a bowl of pottage. Wherever your treasure is, there will be your heart. Political correctness wants your heart, my friends. That's an understatement actually; political correctness demands your heart, your mind, your soul, and your strength. It wants to make it very clear the answers you're looking for, it provides.

Political correctness mimics sacred Scripture to give itself legitimacy by utilizing ethics and virtues of the Bible but recreating them in its godless image. Political correctness makes a big deal about its claim of bringing value, dignity, and justice to the marginalized in society. Blessed are the group identities for they shall inherit the earth.

But God is the one who already told us who we are to love and assist: anyone in need. And notice how God's revelation differs in that there are no races except the human race. Those who cannot provide for themselves, as in widows and orphans, should be helped willingly and sacrificially but certainly not through government coercion.

Because political correctness masks its agenda in philanthropy and justifies it by inculcating our youth in its philosophy through the public educational system, it takes on the appearance of insight and revelation when in fact it's the same tired old mantra Satan launched in the beginning when he said, "I will be like God." Political correctness sets itself up as God and if you refuse to serve it, you will be destroyed.

Think about it. Is there any leniency given in politically correct moments of wokeness? No. Conform or pay. Any opportunity to discuss alternate ideas or perhaps at least allow folks to dissent without repercussions to continue the marvelous gift of free speech given to us in the First Amendment? No.

If your ideas come from Conservative and Christian ideas, they not only are wrong, they are evil. You are marginalized, disinvited from campuses because they can't risk poisoning our youth with the skills of critical thinking and weighing evidence. No, we will do all the thinking for you! We own your thoughts.

What happened to loving the Lord with all your heart, soul, MIND, and strength? We own your bodies. We decide who works where. Competence will take a backseat to quotas. We will choose the marginalized group flavor of the month and they will be given precedence in hiring, school admissions, and government contracts. This will be fair and just and if you don't quite understand the logic, fear not; you don't have to because there is none.

Logic is just patriarchy anyways as it was created by men and used to subjugate the planet but fear not; your salvation is nigh! God made creation male and female so that idea must immediately be deconstructed. We will start by demanding women be treated like men in order for them to be equal. They are so equal, by the way, we will even lower some of the physical standards men must endure to make a more even playing field. Not that women need that, of course, because they are exactly like men, but we will make any concession to give the illusion our point of view is true and works even without pragmatic evidence to prove it.

We don't need any proof because our perception of the utopian society we have created is real because we deem it so. Evidence to the contrary be damned! After we have gotten society to buy in to this new norm we will go even further and create a society that doesn't even acknowledge men and women exist at all. It was a social construct all along and who is this archaic God who so hemmed you into exploring your true self he/she/it would deny you your self-created identity?

Political correctness makes sure you realize if there is a God—fear not—God is YOU! So by lying to the people and forcing the rest of us to adhere we are literally living a lie. Jesus told us Satan is the father of lies and so to be politically correct is to serve a lie. To serve a lie is sin.

Lastly, as I mentioned, there is zero leniency for those who dissent. One of the oddest and most difficult demands the Lord gave us was love your enemies and pray for those who despitefully use you. As much as I want to defame and destroy the new atheists who mock my faith, the politically correct who have hijacked Christian ethics, and the materialists who have made the human race God, I am asked to pray for them.

Another great template for an orthodoxy is not only how it works but if it works. Watching the love and compassion and sacrifice and self-denial used by Christians through the ages to show what a better world can actually look like, we are part of a legacy of freaks. We are strangers in a strange land. We are asked not only to believe in God but to live the supernatural, naturally. We aren't allowed to force our beliefs on anyone nor to hate and exclude those who disagree with us. Politics has nothing to do with who we are, but Jesus does. He is our source for guidance, truth, and being a good neighbor.

To the true believer, no government nor social coercion is necessary. We are duty bound to love our neighbor as ourselves and unlike the politically correct, our neighbor is anyone and everyone in need of a Savior. Even those who hate us and oppose and censor our viewpoints. This is not an easy task; in fact, it is very hard. But hard makes us persevere and perseverance leads to habits which lead to character traits which we pray help guide others to God.

So, yes, Christian, be fair and just and kind. But don't be tolerant. We were never called to simply "tolerate" others; we were commanded to love others as ourselves. That's what sets us apart. That comes with a price, I might add. Jesus promised if you truly believe in Him, you will be hated. Political correctness hates Christians for our belief in moral absolutes. The culture will begin to call your morals a disguise for bigotry. People's autonomy to do what they want without responsibility or shame is the new normal. We will have to fight against that.

When you attempt to inculcate your Christian beliefs into your work or talent or livelihood, you will be sued, ridiculed, and protested. You will be made a pariah in the culture and when Christianity is spoken of it will be defined as the intolerant, bigoted, and hateful philosophy that must be eliminated to bring salvation to America. This is the new normal.

But please keep in mind that one of the main principles political correctness is eliminating is shame. Yet what is shame for? It is to remind us when we are no longer following God's best. Christians have a word for what it creates. Conviction. Shame is designed to bring us to truth. Think of the sobering reality. When you refuse to speak truth to someone for the concern it will hurt their feelings (cause shame in other words) you are literally stealing their soul's access to the means by which God brings them to repentance.

This is just the beginning of the persecution of the Body in America. Christians are now literally the most persecuted religious group on Earth! Yet it is justified under the iron fist of political correctness because, after all, we deserve to be attacked and destroyed. We have the audacity to believe humans owe God their obedience instead of the state.

Here's the good news. You are on a journey and in the middle of the story God wrote just for you. If you are in terrible torment or a season of rest, God has your story completed. We can even cheat a little bit and read the last chapter. No matter what God asks of you on Earth, your story as a Christ follower ends with being in His presence. You will know as you are known. You will see as you are seen. You will spend eternity in absolute joy and completeness. No more tears, no more pain, no more abandonment, no more injustice, no more loss.

Since we not only know how our story ends but that God wants that for all His creation, clearly it is our turn as American believers to sacrifice convenience and safety for the sake of the sinner. There needs to be a third Great Awakening in America and boldness wrapped in love without abandoning truth must carry the day.

I have been in the game for many years now and am not about to quit when I see the finish line in the distance. I didn't get there by being politically correct though, and I urge you to do likewise. I sure covet you coming alongside me as we venture into uncharted territory. Lifting each other and carrying a portion of the load so we can all enter one day into the Holy of Holies, finally unburdened and at rest. Some of the best of us are already there waiting to put an arm around our shoulders and walk with us to our mansion, all the while saying to us, "Now that really wasn't so bad, was it?"

EPILOGUE

What Do I Know?

I wish I were a genius. I would love to think that somehow I am given secret access to the thoughts of God and He trusts me alone to deliver answers to heretofore unanswerable questions. I would like to think when I depart this mortal coil, my words will go on enlightening and encouraging fellow travelers who have simply believed the claims of Jesus to be true.

I guess what I'm saying is I wish I were a C. S. Lewis, for example. He's a hero to me and just to wander around in his mind for a moment would be, I think, a pleasurable experience. But the truth is I'm not nor shall I ever be Mr. Lewis, and I want to take a moment to acknowledge him as an inspiration to me and my thoughts. I also want to tip my hat to a kindred soul I only met in print, the late Bob Briner. I saw a synergistic take on modern Christianity here in the U.S. from Mr. Briner, which he eloquently spoke of years ago in *Roaring Lambs* and *Deadly Detours*, and I believe his work really began getting me thinking about cultural awareness as a Christian artist and my responsibility to redeem it.

Thanks also to the late Chuck Colson and the BreakPoint daily transcripts that have helped shape, define, and inspire my worldview over the years. I have read and incorporated into my comedy show many ideas from the books he has recommended. Also let me acknowledge the works of Nancy Pearcey, and any book she puts out is mandatory reading for the American Christian. She is the most underappreciated philosopher/cultural commentator in the world in my opinion. Also, I want to thank the books and lectures from William Lane Craig, John Lennox, the late Ravi Zacharias, Phillip Johnson, and Stephen Meyer. Also a nod to Alvin Plantinga. I say a nod because everything he writes is so hard to grasp he makes my head explode. There are many more authors and people who have influenced my thinking and meditation and I never stop reading and trying to acquire as much information and insight as I can.

All I have ever wanted as a Conservative comic and a Christian was to be given a place at the table with the rest of the alleged intelligentsia/entertainers of our modern age. I'm a comic with a different point of view than most and I simply ask for a chance to be heard. But, alas, the entertainment world is controlled by a leftist ideology that demands subservience to its worldview and stifles all dissent, in the name of tolerance, no less. I could end this with that last dig at progressive ideology but unfortunately it wouldn't be the complete story.

Even as I wrote these last words years ago before I ever knew this book would get published, I was in the process of being interviewed extensively for a large profile piece being done on me for the *New Yorker* magazine in 2004. A reporter spent days with me, trying to get as much information as he could on this comedian, who is representing a completely unrepresented group of Americans when it comes to comedy: the Conservatives and the Christians. He even followed me to

Estes Park, Colorado, where I performed for a men's retreat. He wanted to see my show live in front of Christians.

After the first of two shows, I waited to talk to the guys and watched a man approach this reporter. He asked if he could speak to him privately, and I knew, of course, that it meant he was going to slam me. After ten minutes I walked up to the two of them and asked how things were going and what they were talking about. As this Christian man began to fumble with his words, he said how he was telling the reporter he didn't like the way I did my show and to also let him know he was a liberal. I glanced down and noticed Adam (the reporter) had his tape recorder on.

What I wanted to ask this brother was why he was so gutless in not approaching me first and talking our issues out between "family," especially if he was the biblical scholar he thought he was. If so, he would know the biblical mandate is to come to me first. Instead, I began to talk and reason with him, all the while biting my lip. I think I found common ground between the two of us. He admitted he laughed at my show; he just disagreed with my style.

Unfortunately (or maybe not?), this discussion had to happen in front of a nonbeliever. There are not many chances for a performer to get profiled in such an esteemed publication as the *New Yorker*, let alone a CHRISTIAN. Obviously, Satan was aware of this as well and wanted to make sure, when the opportunity arose, the world would see what kind of people make up this Body called Christ. Obviously, division is more important to us than reconciliation. Divisions drive us, not our similarities. The Bible said we would be known as Christians by our love for one another; so, apparently, there are only a handful of authentic cases of regenerate lives being led.

For those of you gifted at reading between the lines, you will see the majority of this book was written from pain; pain mainly stemming from fellow believers. I have known my entire walk how bad an example I, too, am as a Christian. I know my foibles and failures and, believe me, that's burden enough without having them driven home by "well-meaning" Christians. I realize, by the way, for many of you reading these pages, I'm not going to change your mind regarding some of the topics discussed. But the truth is, that's not what's most important to me. There are only two objectives, if accomplished, that matter to me as a result of this book.

I pray Christians actually take time to consider seriously their faith and the beliefs their faith gives them, realizing there will always be much more complex and mysterious ways to view our faith than we have usually done. It simply isn't as black and white as we want it to be sometimes.

I hope all Christians begin to create the environment and the habits where we can completely disagree about an element of our faith that is not one of the fundamentals and still love and encourage one another! Could you imagine the power that unity would project!? That's why we'll never see it; disunity is Satan's only weapon in keeping the Christian worldview from literally controlling the nations of the earth! The battle is at hand, and, as long as an equal amount of our warfare is aimed at each other, a lost world has little to fear.

My friends, I have reached a place in my life where I have determined I can no longer live my faith based on how other Christians think I'm supposed to behave. God has made it clear to me He has, believe it or not, endowed me with a prophet's anointing to speak the hard and dangerous truths the American church for the most part is unwilling to receive.

I am literally a missionary to America and those two callings have made me and will continue to make me a maverick in the Christian comedy world.

I have resigned myself to the realization I will be engaging in this fight with God the Father as my King but very few warriors at my side. I have settled in my heart the fact, come hell or high water, I will go to my death proclaiming the Good News that God is real, He loves us all, and He desperately wants a relationship with His creation, and that being said, I will from this day forth take my cues from the Holy Spirit's leading.

I wish I could be everything everyone wants me to be, but I can't. Some of you are just going to have to "Put a Helmet On!" If you don't agree with everything I say, counsel with me. If you don't agree with the way I say it, pray for me. If you're confused by some of my methodology, inquire of me. I am always willing to listen to an honest difference of opinion, but only when that opinion comes from the maturity that delights only in Christ and Him being lifted up.

Love me and partner with me, and maybe we'll actually see a difference in our churches, communities, and culture. If you will do that for me, I promise to give you something in return. Something you will treasure and appreciate for the rest of your life, something that someday you will need desperately and then be eternally grateful it's been given to you. It's extremely rare and when it surfaces it's in short supply. It's something you already have from God but rarely see from man. I promise to give you...

…grace.

ABOUT THE AUTHOR

Brad Stine is known as the man who revolutionized and launched a new era of Christian comedy in America. With his breakout album, *Put A Helmet On!*, he single-handedly redefined Christian stand-up comedy. Brad has thirty years of live performance, film, and television experience.

Brad was a regular live social commentator on *Fox & Friends* every Monday morning for six months. He has been featured in the *New Yorker* magazine, the *New York Times*, the *Christian Science Monitor*, the *Los Angeles Times*, the *Wall Street Journal*, and *USA TODAY*. He has been profiled on *NBC Nightly News*, HBO, Showtime, CNN, *Glenn Beck*, *Hannity & Colmes*, NPR'S *Fresh Air*, ABC's *Nightline* segment "TWICE" (a thirty-minute news show highlighting someone or something in American culture), MTV, and Comedy Central. He has had material published in *Reader's Digest* and *Focus on the Family* magazine. Brad lives with his wife and family in Nashville, Tennessee.

For booking Brad Stine, purchasing his merchandise, or donating to his ministry, please go to www.bradstine.com.